Resolving Grievances:
A Practical Approach

Resolving Grievances:
A Practical Approach

Donald S. McPherson

with Conrad John Gates
and Kevin N. Rogers

HD
6972.5
.M39
1983

Reston Publishing Company, Inc.
Reston, Virginia

228965

Library of Congress Cataloging in Publication Data

McPherson, Donald S.
  Resolving grievances.

  1. Grievance procedures. 2. Grievance arbitration.
3. Grievance procedures—Case studies. 4. Grievance
arbitration—Case studies. I. Gates, Conrad John.
II. Rogers, Kevin N. III. Title.
HD6972.5.M39 1983   331.88'96   82-22993
ISBN 0—8359—6663—1

© 1983 by Reston Publishing Company, Inc.
Reston, Virginia 22090

10 9 8 7 6 5 4 3 2 1

Printed in the United States of America

To Marty, who urged that it be written

To Linda and Kimra, who make everything possible and worthwhile with their love and support

And to Dad, whose animated mealtime stories of the "grieviance man" at the steel mill sparked an early childhood interest.

Contents

Preface

This book grew from my experiences and frustrations in teaching about the process of grievance resolution. In the typical undergraduate collective bargaining course, available texts usually provide materials for practical application only for negotiations, using bargaining games, and for arbitration, using case studies. But while few of the students enrolled are ever likely to negotiate labor agreements or to present arbitration cases, a number are likely to be involved in resolving grievances as supervisors, employee representatives, or, indeed, as grievants. Typically, collective bargaining texts devote little attention to skill building in resolving grievances; collections of simulations are rare.

For graduate courses in contract administration and noncredit training workshops for union and management practitioners, the need for practical teaching materials is even more grave. Theoretical treatment of the grievance procedure in retrospect, from the perspective of arbitration, can be found in abundance, but few sources reverse the focus and treat arbitration from the perspective of grievance resolution. Furthermore, only grievance case simulations, usually in role-play format, can provide the necessary opportunities for building practical skills. Experienced directors of education or training for both management and labor as well as many academicians have developed and collected simulations for this purpose. Indeed, trainers are persistent collectors—and inveterate "borrowers." But few, if any, published collections are available.

What seemed needed, then, was a single source containing general introductory description and theory focused on the grievance-arbitration procedure, together with a collection of role-play simulations on a variety of issues, at differing levels of difficulty or complexity. The narrative portion of this book and the case simulations have been developed over time with that instructional purpose in mind and have been tested both in the academic classroom and the training seminar.

The book specifically does not describe or analyze how grievances actually are processed in most real world labor-management relationships. Indeed, the reader who seeks such description probably will find this work hopelessly idealistic, naive, or simplistic. Rather, an underlying assumption is that far too little training—often none—is given to most supervisors and union stewards in the theory of grievance resolution and even less in the practical human relations, communications, and labor relations skills, which are its art. Too often, at the lower steps at least, grievance meetings are a sham; representatives of the parties are too frequently unsophisticated, inarticulate, or ignorant, through no fault of their own, about this important facet of their responsibilities. Not uncommonly, the representatives understand neither their own roles and those of their counterparts nor the roles of others at different levels in their own organizations. It is easy to find situations where the parties have developed enormous grievance backlogs because virtually all problems rise to the final step of the procedure and periodic horse-trading is the only response to intolerable delay.

We therefore are attempting a practical approach to the process of resolving grievances by providing a source of teaching materials that may contribute to raising the level of skills and knowledge of practitioners. The narrative chapters continuously stress the interrelationships of the various levels of the grievance procedure and the advocates at those levels. We have not hesitated to use words like *should, must,* or *might* to describe alternative courses of action available to the parties. Specific suggestions or prescriptions are offered not only because they are consistent with a theoretical labor relations model but also, more importantly, because they make sense from the selfish, vested interests of the parties.

Both the narrative portions and the simulations have been used successfully with undergraduate students, graduate students, and supervisors and stewards in training workshops. We have tried to provide enough straightforward information and theoretical depth so that the various chapters can be used as a complete discussion of a topic or merely as an introduction to it, depending upon the level of the class. With some groups, the introductory material may be slightly too theoretical; the instructor may want to highlight essential points through questions and discussions. At other levels, the instructor may have to supply more advanced, supplementary materials.

The case simulations can be used in a variety of ways. If time is not available for role playing a certain case, for instance, that case might simply be read by the class and then discussed. The cases are developed as role descriptions for second- or third-step grievance meetings, but they contain enough information to be used for first-step meetings and, after simulating the grievance procedure, for arbitration preparation and presentation. Because they are role plays, the cases serve as a vehicle for developing not only conceptual labor relations knowledge but also behavioral skills in communications and human relations. The instructor may want to introduce a case with a discussion of topics such as leadership style, feedback,

xiii
Preface

effective discipline, or "active" listening, or the simulation can be used to develop shared experiences that will introduce such a discussion.

It is effective when a single group acts out the simulation in front of the class—or more usefully, with the rest of a class circled around the participants—and then the class critiques the "performance." An alternative is to require the entire class to be prepared to play all of the roles or assign specific roles to particular groups, so that as the grievance progresses from step to step, some "actors" can leave their roles and be replaced by others from the "audience." Two formats can be used to involve all the students in the same case simultaneously. In a large room, as many as five or six groups can role play the same case, with the instructor acting as a floating observer and facilitator. Alternatively, the role of observer-critic can be added to each simulation so that each group has several students participating unobtrusively; their role would be to observe carefully and later to supply criticism and reflection.

The case simulations are most valuable if the instructor has the time to build a sense of group consciousness in the class, perhaps using some team-building exercises, if the participants are not already a self-perceived group. If a sufficiently open relationship is established between the participants, learning effectiveness can be increased enormously by following the simulation with the participants criticizing each other en role. Grievants can report to stewards how they feel about the representation they received. Stewards can share feelings about the problems of getting enough information. Union representatives can report their perceptions about the fairness of the meeting to management representatives, who can tell labor relations directors how they felt about their role within the management organization. Depending on the instructor's goals and available time, group discussion also can be focused on body language, empathetic response, and effective presentation.

In general, participants should be encouraged or directed to play unaccustomed roles. Foremen should play personnel directors; international representatives should play shop stewards. In joint training, union and management participants should reverse their usual roles. Following the simulation itself and a discussion of the performances en role, there should be a general discussion of labor relations principles. Alternatives to the decisions during the simulation can be discussed, as well as the prospects for each party with arbitration. If a number of groups experience the simulation simultaneously, a concluding, large group discussion revealing similarities and differences in the handling of the same case by different people can be extremely enlightening. Indeed, with respect to learning effectiveness for the participants, it is impossible to emphasize too strongly to instructors the necessity of allowing sufficient time for completely processing the group experience.

Finally, the simulations have not been designed to produce performances amenable to grading, while it is no doubt possible to do so. Role plays enhance self-learning to the extent that they are followed by specific and descriptive feedback, introspection, and reflection.

Donald S. McPherson

Acknowledgments

Jack Gates and Kevin Rogers have contributed invaluably to this project. Many months ago, Jack somewhat reluctantly agreed to provide a short chapter on arbitration. Ultimately, his enthusiastic contribution included not only two outstanding chapters dealing with the theoretical and applied facets of that topic drawn from his years of experience as a lawyer, advocate, arbitrator, and instructor but also countless hours devoted to discussing, criticizing, and editing the entire work. Kevin read endless arbitration awards in order to construct the plot outlines for the simulations according to what must have seemed incredibly perplexing instructions from me. Many hours were devoted to brainstorming standard principles to be illustrated, researching awards, developing circumstances, adding characterization, and constructing materials that could be used successfully in the classroom. He also brought his considerable editorial skills to the task of criticizing the entire work.

Martin Morand made the original declaration that the book must be written and also provided an enormously valuable critique both of the narrative and of the simulations from the perspective of his years of experience as a union advocate, labor educator, and instructor. Our colleague at IUP, Thomas Sedwick, participated in many of the group discussions that led to presentation of particular concepts. Walter Gershenfeld of Temple University provided a most useful critique of the original idea. Paul Hoffner, Frederick Nesbitt, and Robert Gaylor all reacted to the material in earlier forms and provided helpful suggestions.

Christina Meyers typed and edited much of the draft. Linda McPherson proofread and edited all of it. It is impossible to be sufficiently grateful for the many hours spent in these tasks.

Finally, to our students, who have been and will continue to serve as guinea pigs for this material, we express our appreciation and hope that their own skills and insight have grown from the experience.

PART I

AMERICAN INDUSTRIAL JURISPRUDENCE: THE GRIEVANCE-ARBITRATION PROCESS

Donald S. McPherson
Conrad John Gates

CHAPTER 1

Introduction

The collective bargaining agreement, also referred to as the contract or labor agreement, is a unique feature of the industrial relations system that has developed in the United States since passage of the National Labor Relations Act in 1935. The contract is a written agreement between an employer and a union that represents all employees in a bargaining unit, concerning the employment relationship and the manner in which work will be performed. More specific details of the employment relationship are negotiated in a typical American collective bargaining agreement than in any other labor agreement virtually anywhere in the world. In other nations, in fact, it is far more common for labor and management not to work under a written contract at all. But in the United States the familiar trilogy of mandatory bargaining issues—wages, hours, and other terms and conditions of employment—encompasses an enormous area within which the parties can create their relationship.

COLLECTIVE BARGAINING: AN ADVERSARIAL SYSTEM

The American system of industrial relations is built on the assumption that there is a natural and legitimate divergence of interests between employers and employees concerning wages, hours, and working conditions. In the simplest terms, the divergence is natural because employers view most changes in wages, hours, and working conditions that are favorable to employees as costs that reduce potential profits or, in other settings, increase the cost of services provided. Collective bargaining does not attempt to eliminate the conflict inherent in this divergence of interests. Instead, collective bargaining assumes that the conflict is natural and, through the contract, seeks to establish a framework to deal with conflict in a rational, predictable, and peaceful manner.

The objective of providing for collective bargaining as a national public policy, then, is to channel labor-management conflict into peaceful resolution by providing for the equality of both parties and protecting the legitimate interests of both the employer and the union. Bargaining is, by its nature, an adversarial process involving proposals and counterproposals, compromise, trading, and, most essentially, the exercise of various forms of power. Even within a deliberately structured adversary relationship, nothing prevents the parties from cooperating to the fullest measure consistent with their short- and long-range interests. Indeed, an employer and union may have sufficient mutual interests to lead toward cooperation in a wide variety of areas. Nevertheless, the decision to cooperate springs from a relationship that is inherently competitive. The process of negotiation forges an accord out of the inherent conflict between the parties; the written agreement represents the practical, operational details of the accord.

Once a union is certified as the exclusive bargaining agent for an employee bargaining unit, the union and employer incur a mutual legal obligation to meet and confer in good faith with respect to wages, hours, and other terms and conditions of employment, i.e., a duty to bargain. While neither party is compelled by law to make or accept any specific proposals or to reach agreement at all, each is required to negotiate in good faith with the intent to reach agreement. If an agreement is reached, moreover, it must be reduced to writing and signed by the parties. As the product of a contractual relationship based upon voluntary agreement, the contract is enforceable in a court of law, and each party has the obligation to ensure that the agreement is implemented properly. Under the law, the duty to bargain extends not only to the negotiation of a collective agreement but also to the negotiated settlement of any disputes concerning its meaning while it is in force. Thus, collective bargaining is a continuous process, adversarial in nature, which begins with contract negotiation, flows through the resolution of disputes under the agreement, and extends to the negotiation of successor agreements.

ROLES OF THE PARTIES

In the most commonly accepted model of labor-management relations, the responsibility of management, representing the employer, is to implement the agreement; the responsibility of the union is to police or enforce it. This model arises directly from the nature of the employment relationship. Management generally is the acting party; it represents an employer who hires, directs, disciplines, promotes, and fires employees. The union's objective in bargaining is to secure contract language that limits the employer's otherwise virtually unfettered right to take such actions unilaterally. Unless faced with the duty to bargain with a certified union, management is limited only by restrictions imposed in law and by those that it voluntarily imposes upon itself. Thus, when a union concludes an agreement with an employer through a process requiring *joint* determination of the fundamental aspects of the employment relationship, the union wins rights that were previously management's sole prerogative. If management naturally assumes the role of implementing the agreement because it is typically the acting party, the union naturally assumes the role of policing management's implementation in order to enforce the rights that it has secured.

The mechanism through which the two parties interact in their complementary contract administration roles is the grievance-arbitration procedure. The grievance procedure functions as a system of industrial jurisprudence, that is, as a process with a formal set of rules and procedures to identify disputes between the parties; to process them, including appeals; and to provide for final resolution under the terms of the collective bargaining agreement. Unlike the meaning of jurisprudence in its legal context, however, industrial jurisprudence as represented in the grievance-arbitration procedure is entirely private. The parties agree between themselves how to handle disputes concerning the agreement. They can negotiate a grievance procedure concluding with binding arbitration and write that procedure into their contract; the vast majority of collective agreements contain such negotiated grievance procedures. On the other hand, the parties can choose not to provide a mechanism for handling disputes; in this case they are left to their own devices. In some basic trades, for example, negotiated grievance procedures are not common; disputes may involve job actions, including strikes, before they are eventually settled. In contrast a grievance-arbitration procedure provides for final resolution not through the exercise of power but through the determination of a neutral third party, an arbitrator. The only role for the courts in such a private system of industrial jurisprudence is to serve as guarantor of the contract by ensuring that the parties utilize the process stipulated in the labor agreement.

At each stage in the grievance-arbitration procedure, the union makes its charges, attempts to substantiate the allegations, and tries to persuade management to grant the relief sought by the union or to agree to a mutually acceptable compromise solution. Similarly, management at each stage must defend its actions against the charges and then allow the grievance, negotiate a settlement, or reject the grievance. If no resolution is reached during the internal stages of the appeals process, the union may appeal the employer's rejection to a neutral third party, an arbitrator, whose decision will be final and binding upon the parties as long as the provisions in question remain in the agreement. Since each employer and union are free to tailor their own, private dispute resolution mechanism, the "system" of industrial jurisprudence is decentralized and highly individualized. It is a system not in the sense that the courts represent a unified legal system of jurisprudence but rather in the sense that most of the individual grievance-arbitration procedures are similar in their essential nature. Just as the collective bargaining agreement that establishes the grievance-arbitration procedure is uniquely American, the system of industrial jurisprudence created by collective bargaining agreements is a distinguishing feature of industrial relations in the United States.

Why should the parties agree to an internal system for resolving any disputes regarding the contract? From the employer's standpoint, risking a suit to enforce the contract or a strike for every union complaint would introduce enormous instability and a significant threat to efficient production. From the union's standpoint, having to go to court or to call a strike for every complaint would produce grave political problems, since employees must agree to strike, or involve potentially huge legal costs. Thus, the employer's primary objective in agreeing to a grievance-arbitration procedure is securing a no-strike pledge for the term of the agreement in exchange. In giving up its right to strike, the union's primary objective is to guarantee that its rights won in the contract can be enforced by a neutral third party beyond the employer's authority. Each party, then, compromises its most fundamental right. The union gives up its only tool of economic power to influence the employer during the term of the agreement; the employer gives up the right as the final judge in the most significant areas of the employment policy.

Arbitration, the final step of the grievance procedure, represents both a protection for the parties of their fundamental concerns and an incentive to settle disputes before they reach the final step. Management's protection is the more immediate: a grievance procedure ensures that work will continue, subject to managerial authority, even while that authority is challenged. Management's actions are not held in abeyance pending the appeal through the grievance procedure. Thus, the common law of the shop is that an employee must obey now and grieve later. A refusal to submit to management's direction may be a capital offense, insubordination, which is subject to capital punishment, discharge. If it is ultimately decided that management acted improperly, its authority will be clarified and grievants will be made whole for any losses suffered. A union can hardly expect to negate an employer's inherent authority to manage the enterprise and to direct the work force simply by lodging a complaint that must be proven; its protection necessarily must be less immediate than the employer's. But the ultimate protection of mandatory third-party enforcement of the contract is highly significant compared with the financial and political costs of the alternatives.

The inherent disincentive for exercising the ultimate protection of arbitration is the great uncertainty and risk for each party. An arbitrator may know nothing about the parties, their relationship, and their problems prior to an arbitration hearing and thus may fail to understand the intricacies and implications of a dispute. The arbitrator may be fully capable of understanding, but the parties may fail to explain the dispute clearly. A wide variety of other factors—human frailty, unclear testimony by witnesses, procedural problems—can turn an arbitration award into a disaster for either party. Management may be directed to take some action that is exceedingly costly or disruptive to its preferred practices. The union may lose a right that it believed it had won and have no recourse for the duration of the agreement because of its no-strike pledge. Except when an arbitrator is found to have exceeded his or her authority to settle disputes under the contract or to have been guilty of malfeasance, an award will be final and binding upon the parties. Courts will not second-guess an arbitrator's conclusions if he or she reached them properly within his or her authority. Instead, they will enforce the contract by ordering that the parties get exactly what they bargained for, the final and binding decision of the third party of their choice.

Thus, at its final stage, the grievance-arbitration procedure represents great uncertainty; it is both a protection for and risk to each party's most basic interests. In its earlier stages, the procedure also represents a creative vehicle through which, if they have the will, the parties may choose to negotiate a resolution to their dispute that protects their fundamental interests without introducing the uncertainty of arbitration.

MANAGEMENT RIGHTS

As noted, an employer has certain inherent management rights originating in the condition of being an employer. For example, if an employer engages employees for some purpose, that employer must have the right to hire, direct the work force, and determine what work will be done and in what manner. In addition, employers were traditionally considered to possess a virtually unlimited reservoir of "reserved rights." If, in the absence of collective bargaining, all rights were vested in management except those limited by law, then it is logical, from an employer's viewpoint, that management must retain all rights except those it explicitly surrenders in the collective bargaining agreement. From this perspective, if a labor agreement had no language whatever addressing the rights of management, management would still have all rights, including rights never previously exercised or even yet conceived, except those specifically limited by contract language. For a considerable period, even after collective bargaining became supported and encouraged as public policy in 1935, the reserved rights theory was logical and persuasive to most courts and arbitrators.

As collective bargaining expanded and grievance-arbitration procedures matured, however, the reserved rights theory underwent a significant transformation. Unions argued that if they gave up their right to strike during the term of a collective agreement, then favorable practices and conditions in effect prior to the agreement should remain in effect unless they were the subject of negotiation. If management intended to change such conditions, unions argued, the union should have been advised during negotiations in order to take those factors into account in developing its bargaining strategy and positions. Thus, a recognition grew both at arbitration and in the courts that existing practices should be included within the scope of a union's contractually protected rights even though they may not be explicitly covered in the language of the contract.

This recognition fatally damaged the reserved rights theory. If management wanted to secure protection for the widest possible prerogatives, its most reasonable choice became negotiating explicit management rights clauses in agreements. But if such clauses are negotiable, then management would have to bargain for a satisfactory statement of its rights; that course of action implicitly recognizes that the employer must not possess an unlimited reservoir of rights permitting complete freedom of action except for contractual restrictions.

Moreover, arbitrators and courts gradually concluded that a labor agreement also contains many implied limitations on management's rights. For example, if a contract provides for promotion on the basis of seniority, assuming that the bidder has the ability to do the job, the contract also implies maintenance of a reasonable stability in established positions. In other words, if seniority as the basis for promotions were negotiated in good faith, with the reference point being a set of circumstances then in effect, the employer should not be able to undermine the effect of the agreement later by arbitrarily changing the job descriptions of positions and then assigning duties at random. Similarly, if an employer recognizes a union as the exclusive representative of a bargaining unit that contains certain specific positions, thereby implying the existence of bargaining unit work, the employer should not then be able arbitrarily to undercut the unit later by eliminating positions and assigning the duties to another group of employees not in the unit or to an outside contractor. This is not to say that management does not possess the rights to establish job descriptions or to contract out work. Rather, management's rights in such areas are not absolute when a labor agreement is in effect. Whether management possesses certain rights in specific situations is a matter to be resolved by the grievance-arbitration procedure under the agreement.

Thus, while it is not accurate to say that management rights include only inherent management rights plus whatever rights are specifically reserved to management in the express language of the agreement, it is also not accurate to say that management possesses both its inherent rights and all those rights not explicitly surrendered in the agreement. The effect of the Supreme Court's famous *Steelworkers Trilogy* decisions in 1960, which are discussed in some detail in later chapters, was official recognition of negotiated grievance-arbitration procedures as the primary mechanism for resolving challenges to management authority under a collective bargaining agreement.[1]

UNION RIGHTS

The preceding discussion of management rights implies a great deal about the nature of union rights. While management enters negotiations with its inherent right to manage by virtue of being an employer, a union enters with only the right to bargain. Obviously a union possesses whatever rights it can secure in a contract through negotiations. Since the duty to bargain requires neither party to make or accept any specific proposal, a union could potentially secure few or extensive rights depending partly on its bargaining skill and power. Furthermore, while the parties are only obligated to negotiate about wages, hours, and working conditions, they may negotiate about anything else that they wish. For example, unions commonly achieve the right to use bulletin boards for union business or to use the employer's internal mail system. It is also possible for the union to secure enormously powerful rights with respect to its security as the bargaining agent if the employer agrees. A contract can establish a union shop, that is, employees must join the union as a condition of employment once they have completed a specified period. Moreover, as discussed earlier, a union secures certain implied rights when it concludes a collective bargaining agreement, such as the right to grieve to protect the integrity of the bargaining unit despite the absence of express language to that effect.

In addition to contractual rights, the union has the legal right to function as the exclusive representative of the employees in the bargaining unit that it represents. Thus, the union may insist that the employer deal with it alone in all matters related to collective bargaining and the bargaining unit. This means that the employer may not deal with individuals, independent groups, or other unions concerning such subjects. The National Labor Relations Act does provide that employees may take grievances directly to management without intervention by the union, but the union has the right to be present for any "adjustment" of such grievances, though not to participate.[2]

A union has the right, indeed the obligation, to enforce the contract. The National Labor Relations Board has consistently ruled that by implication a union has the right to secure all information reasonably necessary to its grievance responsibilities and that the employer must supply such information promptly and in reasonably useful form upon a good faith demand by the union.[3] Too frequently union representatives fail to appreciate the importance of this right, which arises from the union's status as an equal party in the administration of the contract. Often unions fail to insist upon receiving from management information necessary to evaluate and prepare a grievance; even if they do insist, many managers are not fully aware of the extent of the union's right to information.

Obviously a union that negotiates and then supervises a grievance-arbitration procedure under a collective agreement has the right to represent grievants in the procedure. Arbitrators have frequently ruled that unions must have wide latitude in their contract enforcement activities as a right implied in the agreement. Similarly arbitrators usually hold that the union has a contractually implied right, distinct from its legal right, to secure information reasonably related to its grievance activities. However, these implied rights are not unlimited; labor agreements frequently define the latitude of union representatives in conducting grievance investigations on work time, for example. As the enforcer of the contract, the union also has the implied right to file grievances on its own initiative and to agree to grievance settlements independent of the views of affected employees. In general, just as the union may not interfere with the employer's fundamental right to manage the organization, the employer may not interfere with the union's fundamental right to conduct its representational functions in the manner that it deems appropriate. Disputes regarding these rights may be subject to charges of unfair practice before a labor board or to grievances, or to both.

INDIVIDUAL EMPLOYEE RIGHTS

Legal status as the exclusive representative for all employees in the bargaining unit represents a considerable endowment of power for a union. Through a series of Supreme Court decisions, this power has been tempered with significant obligations. Beginning with *Steele* v. *Louisville & Nashville R.R.* (1944) and continuing through such signal cases as *Vaca* v. *Sipes* (1967) and *Hines* v. *Anchor Motor Freight* (1976), the Supreme Court has enunciated a duty of fair representation that the union owes to each bargaining unit member.[4] The concept of exclusivity is the origin for the fair representation duty. If a bargaining unit member has only the union as guarantor of the employee's rights under the contract, the court has held that the union must be required to represent all employees fairly.

In its clearest statement of the fair representation duty, the court said in *Vaca* v. *Sipes* that a union must not act in a manner that is arbitrary, discriminatory, or in bad faith. Thus, a union that fails to pursue an employee's grievance because of the employee's leadership of a rival union political faction or because of the employee's race, breaches its duty. Such a violation may be charged by an individual employee both as an unfair practice and as a lawsuit against the union, from which the employee may collect damages if victorious. Furthermore, in *Hines* v. *Anchor Motor Freight* the court added the criterion of negligence. If a union processes an employee's grievance in a slipshod manner by failing to file it within contractual time limits and the grievance is thereby rejected, the union may be held liable for breach of the fair representation duty. Individual bargaining unit members, whether or not they are actually members of the union, therefore have powerful protective rights against union abuse of its status as exclusive representative.

As noted, individual employees have the right to be represented by the union in the grievance procedure; also the law protects their rights not to be represented in grievance proceedings if they reject union participation. In its *Weingarten* decision in 1975, the Supreme Court enunciated the right of an individual employee to insist on union representation in an investigatory interview if the employee believes that disciplinary action against him or her might reasonably result from the interview.[5] Since such interviews are not formally part of the grievance procedure in which employees clearly have the right to be represented, *Weingarten* represents an important protection of individual rights in the collective bargaining setting. For example, employees of a nonunion employer obviously possess no similar right to be represented. But the right is clearly an individual one that can be exercised or waived by the employee and cannot be invoked by the union. Additionally, neither a union nor an employer can interfere with an employee's statutory rights, such as the right not to be discriminated against in employment on the basis of race, color, sex, religion, or national origin. Nor can an employer obstruct certain civil rights, such as the right to refuse a directive that would cause the employee to commit an illegal act or that poses serious threat to life or health. Finally, although beyond the scope of this book, it should be noted that the Labor-Management Reporting and Disclosure Act (Landrum-Griffin Act) of 1959 established a number of significant rights for union members vis-à-vis their union.[6]

It should be clear from this introductory discussion that a fundamental component of collective bargaining involves the establishment of rights—for the union and employer especially but also for individual employees. Just enforcement of such rights requires that when they come into conflict, a system of regular rules and procedures be available to balance the equities and adjudicate the dispute. As the cornerstone of the American system of industrial jurisprudence, the grievance-arbitration process performs this function. The following chapters discuss in detail the nature of grievances and of arbitration and the functioning of the grievance-arbitration process.

Reference Notes

[1] *United Steelworkers of America* v. *American Manufacturing Co.*, 363 U.S. 564 (1960); *United Steelworkers of America* v. *Enterprise Wheel & Car Corp.*, 363 U.S. 593 (1960); *United Steelworkers of America* v. *Warrior & Gulf Navigation Co.*, 363 U.S. 574 (1960).

[2] National Labor Relations Act; 49 Stat. 449 (1935), § 8 (d).

[3] For a thorough discussion of the right to information, see Charles J. Morris, ed., *The Developing Labor Law* (Washington, D.C.: Bureau of National Affairs, 1971), 309-316.

[4] *Steele* v. *Louisville & Nashville R.R.*, 323 U.S. 192 (1944); *Vaca* v. *Sipes*, 386 U.S. 171 (1967); *Hines* v. *Anchor Motor Freight, Inc.*, 424 U.S. 554 (1976).

[5] *NLRB* v. *Weingarten*, 420 U.S. 251 (1975).

[6] Labor-Management Reporting and Disclosure Act (Landrum-Griffin Act) 73 Stat. 519 (1959).

CHAPTER 2

What Is a Grievance?

Ironically, despite the importance of the grievance procedure in collective bargaining, there is no standard definition of a grievance and no general agreement on its description in a contract. Yet there is widespread agreement among managers, union leaders, neutrals, and industrial relations experts that the definition of a grievance in a labor agreement is fundamental to any collective bargaining relationship. The one definition to which all parties would subscribe seems far from definite in its practical guidance: *a grievance is whatever the parties say that it is.*

The vast majority of collective bargaining agreements in the United States contain grievance-arbitration procedures. Although the parties may agree during negotiations to a specific grievance definition, it is not at all uncommon for a contract simply to describe how a grievance will be handled by outlining the procedure to be followed, rather than to stipulate a specific definition. Even if the parties decide to define a grievance explicitly, there are many choices.

Should only formal complaints constitute grievances, or might they be informal gripes as well? Must a complaint be written or filed before it becomes a grievance, or is it a grievance as soon as a manager is notified orally of the problem? Should grievances be restricted to the explicit language of the contract? Should they also include allegations that the agreement's spirit or intent was violated or that its terms were applied in an arbitrary or otherwise improper fashion? Should alleged violations of statutes or government regulations be included as grievable? Are plant rules and regulations, procedures, dress codes, and codes of conduct grievable? What about unfair treatment? Should management be able to file grievances and process them to arbitration? What are the rights of individual employees in processing grievances? The words chosen at the bargaining table to describe the grievance-arbitration procedure may have enormous influence on the nature of the union-management relationship.

CONTRACTUAL GRIEVANCE DEFINITIONS

It is a fair assumption that the union will seek that combination of explicit contract language and latitude for action that gives the most expansive breadth to the concept of a grievance. When the union gives up its right to strike for the term of the agreement in exchange for a grievance-arbitration procedure, it limits its power to actions that can legitimately be taken under that procedure to enforce the contract. From the union's perspective, any issue relevant to the employment relationship should be grievable. Even with the ability to take disputes beyond management to a neutral arbitrator for resolution, the union can afford to take only a relatively small number of meritorious grievances to the arbitration step.

It may seem equally apparent that management should take precisely the opposite view; that is, a grievance should be defined explicitly and narrowly, and only allegations of specific contract violations should be subject to the procedure. Indeed, such a view does make considerable strategic sense since the union will seek a broad definition. No matter what it ultimately decides about contract language preferences, management will nearly always have a more restrictive view of the scope of grievances than the union. The collective bargaining agreement itself is a severe limitation on management's rights if employees were unorganized. Therefore, to the degree that the ability to grieve management actions may expand the union's prerogatives, the grievance procedure contains the potential for further limitations on management. As a result, management will seek generally to limit the scope of the union's ability to challenge its authority through grievances.

Still, there are quite substantial reasons why an employer might agree to a broad or even liberal grievance definition. Trading broader grievance language for some important union concession at the bargaining table is one obvious possibility. But even beyond bargaining considerations, management gains significant advantages when it takes the serious step of agreeing to subject its actions to review in the grievance process with binding arbitration at its conclusion. First, and most obviously, it gains stability. It can deliver services or maintain production for the term of the agreement with confidence, knowing that there will be no interruptions and no need for unnecessary customer stockpiling. Production will continue while disputes are being worked out through the procedure because, as the Supreme Court decided in the *Boys Markets* case in 1970, an employer can seek an injunction in federal district court to halt a strike when "a collective bargaining contract contains a mandatory grievance adjustment or arbitration procedure."[1] Then, too, there are issues of public relations image, general community good will, and employee satisfaction to consider.

In addition, management gains a system of order within the organization that regularly and rapidly identifies employee problems and presents them for consideration and resolution at the earliest opportunity. Problems will not be left to fester, injuring morale and compromising production or quality of service. Further, management gains the services of the union itself in maintaining employee discipline. The union, which generally controls access to the grievance-arbitration procedure, will have to review complaints and decide which it believes are strong, which are questionable, and which are without merit. Whatever the grievance definition, the union will have to explain to some dissatisfied employees that their complaints may not be strong, or even valid, grievances. The employer also knows that the union will be able to afford arbitration for only a small number of its most important grievances. For the remainder, management's response at the last internal step of the grievance procedure will decide the issue.

Thus, management might agree to a somewhat more expansive grievance definition than a superficial examination of its interests might suggest. Whatever strategic and tactical concerns the employer and union bring to negotiations, an exceedingly important component of the bargain will be discussion about the description of the grievance-arbitration procedure. Whatever they decide, the grievance-arbitration section is one area of the agreement in which they can least afford to take blindly someone else's model or to be careless in their choice of words.

As important as explicit contract language is, however, the parties also define grievable issues by their actions. If the contract does not provide a specific definition or if the definition provided is ambiguous, the practice of the parties will play a crucial role in determining whether a dispute is grievable. As an arbitrator might state it, practice informs the meaning of the contract when the agreement is silent or ambiguous. Even if the agreement defines a grievance with some specificity, practice may still be a key ingredient. The concept of a grievance, therefore, is best illustrated as a continuum. At the most restrictive end, a grievance may be specifically limited to alleged violations of the express terms of the collective bargaining agreement, and all other complaints or disputes would be dealt with as something other than formal grievances. At the least restrictive end, any dispute may be grievable and subject to the procedure. Through their choice of language and their actions, the parties determine the range of issues grievable under their contract.

Moreover, the parties must choose which disputes will be arbitrable and how arbitration will function. Generally, only official grievances can be arbitrated, so only issues considered valid grievances are subject to the arbitration clause. The parties can decide to process all disputes or complaints through the grievance procedure but to define formal grievances as allegations of contract violations and permit only formal grievances to go to the final step of binding arbitration. It is also quite possible to exclude specific types of disputes from arbitration. A contract might provide that an employee may grieve a promotion decision only for himself or herself and only for failure to follow the procedures in the agreement. In this instance, the merits of a promotion decision would not be grievable or subject to arbitration. By using the grievance procedure for all disputes but carefully defining the kinds of issues that are formal grievances, the parties can ensure that common complaints will be confronted and resolved in an orderly and expeditious fashion rather than dismissed on technical grounds because they are not valid grievances.

In addition to defining arbitrability, the parties may wish to specify how an arbitrator will be selected. Sometimes they may agree on a permanent arbitrator or panel of arbitrators. Frequently they will wish to choose a new arbitrator for each case; they must determine not only the source, such as the American Arbitration Association or the Federal Mediation and Conciliation Service, but also the specific method of selection. The parties also want to specify the qualifications of acceptable arbitrators, particularly with respect to disputes that may require considerable technical knowledge. Perhaps most importantly, they probably will want to describe the authority of the arbitrator to settle disputes and order remedies. Agreements typically limit the arbitrator's powers only to the dispute in question and forbid adding to, subtracting from, or in any way changing the contract. The contract language in the arbitration clause is particularly important because if one party or the other believes that a dispute is not arbitrable, an arbitrator must decide that question first before considering the merits of the issue.

To the hypothetical question, Do I have a grievance? there can be only one correct answer: It depends. The question of whether a grievance is winnable is an entirely separate issue. A dispute may be grievable but not winnable. If this uncertainty provides for great frustration, it also provides for great flexibility and allows considerable creativity in addressing problems between the union and management. The grievance-arbitration process is one of the most important arenas in which the parties daily define their relationship.

REASONS FOR GRIEVANCES

Although the grievance-arbitration procedure provides a mechanism for the resolution of disputes regardless of cause, the reasons for or causes of particular grievances frequently influence how well the procedure works. It is not unusual for contract language itself to be the cause of grievances. Questions naturally arise as to why. After all, both parties participated actively in negotiations, should know the meaning of their own words, and should have discussed interpretation problems while bargaining. All too often, insufficient time is spent during bargaining in exploring the implications of language through examples, with the result that the parties bring to the problem of interpretation their own individual frames of reference. But no matter how much time is spent discussing examples for the application of hypothetical contract language in negotiations, unforeseen situations still arise. *Intent* in negotiations has reference only to a meeting of the minds, a bargain, between the parties. The touchstone for interpretation is their *collective* intention when they negotiated a particular phrase or section. Thus, the focus of contract interpretation is not the intent of each party individually when language was negotiated. If collective intent cannot be found, the language might not truly reflect a meeting of the minds. In such cases, substantial differences can quite easily arise and lead to grievances.

Furthermore, the parties are sometimes unable to agree to each other's particular proposal, but the contested issue is not sufficiently important to impede agreement on the entire contract. As a result, they may agree to compromise language that does not directly address the dispute remaining between them. Suppose that the union proposes that stewards be permitted to participate in grievance investigations and meetings on work time, arguing that the resolution of such problems is the legitimate work of both parties. Suppose further that the employer agrees in principle but the parties are unable to agree on the amount of time that a steward might properly spend processing grievances. Instead, they agree to language that permits stewards to spend "a reasonable amount of time" investigating grievances on the job. Such a compromise, and others like it using phrases such as *due consideration* or *appropriate regard for,* allow the parties to reach agreement while leaving to the grievance procedure the specific disputes that may occur when the compromise language is applied.

In addition to deliberate ambiguity, the parties may agree to language that seems clear when bargained but later seems quite equivocal. Often this occurs when hurried agreement in principle is reached on a number of outstanding issues just before a contract expires or when one party agrees to draft large sections of specific language to support general agreements reached at the bargaining table.

Parties may also simply assign different meaning to the same language since they might have reached agreement with different sorts of applications in mind. Unanticipated events or new conditions not addressed at all in negotiations may arise. In these instances, too, the grievance procedure probably will be the mechanism by which the rights and prerogatives of the employee, the union, and management will be determined.

Besides disputes over interpretation of contract language, grievances may arise because of interpersonal relationships. An interpersonal conflict between a supervisor and an employee or group of employees might lead to a grievance that alleges unfair treatment or to a contention that a disciplinary action was not for just cause. Competitive relationships between supervisors or failure of supervisors to coordinate with each other effectively can also lead to disparate treatment of employees or inconsistent enforcement of rules or procedures. Similarly, political or personal differences between union officials can lead to a competition that spills over into the grievance procedure if stewards try to demonstrate their effectiveness by amassing a grievance record. Among employees, in formal or informal work groups, interpersonal problems can lead to grievances that actually reflect disputes among themselves.

As the party responsible for implementing the agreement, management's attitude may lead to grievances. A union might deliberately pursue numerous grievances on technicalities in response to an objectionable management action justified by a narrow or technical construction of the management rights clause. Management may not have taken sufficient care to ensure that all supervisors understand the contract and implement its provisions similarly or to explain management's overall attitudes and objectives in labor relations. Inconsistency is a major cause of grievances and a frequent reason for reversals of disciplinary action by arbitrators.

As the party responsible for enforcing the agreement, the union also may be the cause of grievances. As it responds to problems or complaints, the union may become overzealous in its policing role. Often, insufficient training is given to stewards who then act on their own without proper knowledge of the contract or who use their positions to harass supervisors or to aggravate interpersonal problems. Further, a union with an unstable, divided, hostile membership may be constantly filing grievances in order to demonstrate its influence and activity to employees. The union must take an active role in championing employee grievances. While management is the acting party, the union is the reacting party. Because it probably surrendered its right to strike for the term of the agreement in exchange for the grievance-arbitration process, the union must always test the strength of the contract, to stretch its terms to cover as many issues as possible in addition to those directly addressed and those covered by past practice. Once it gives up the right to strike, the union limits its policing activites to the grievance arena.

There is no escaping the reality that the grievance procedure is a political mechanism for the union vis-à-vis its members and potential members. As the exclusive bargaining agent, to which employees pay dues, the union is always subject to the timeworn question of the worker, What have you done for me lately? Since contracts might only be negotiated every two or three years, with much of the language remaining the same after some initial years of experience, the union must use the grievance procedure to press its interpretation of employee rights secured in the contract. Moreover, the union's attempts to define or widen, if possible, the control of employees over their working conditions through the grievance procedure must be publicized to the membership. Thus, the bargaining agent will publish in the union newsletter stories about rights won from management, about grievances won, and about situations of which employees should be wary. The union's grievance record is the easiest, most visible way for it to demonstrate activity to the membership. Therefore, some grievances may come into the process for purely political reasons unrelated to their merit, as judged by contract language.

Nor are supervisors immune from political pressures within management's organization. A supervisor might set out to demonstrate "toughness" by being intransigent or antagonistic toward the union and not caring how many grievances are filed. Management could decide to pursue a hard line, letting the union file as many grievances as it wants, denying them all, and leaving it to the union to decide how many it can afford to send to arbitration. In the meantime, with a no-strike agreement in place and insubordination a major offense, the employees are in the position of having to obey now and grieve later. Thus, while management may willingly be inundated with grievances, the work will go on until the matters in dispute are resolved to the contrary, probably at arbitration.

Sometimes the mechanism for using the grievance process is the cause of grievances or a factor impeding their resolution. Many grievance procedures provide for an initial informal step during which the problem is discussed and, if possible, solved before becoming a formal, written grievance. A requirement that grievances must be written at the initial step may make resolution of some problems difficult because written records tend to harden positions, promote characterization of motives, and foster self-justification among those involved. Even more importantly, representatives at the lower steps—shop committee members or stewards for the union and foremen or supervisors for management—frequently do not have the authority to resolve problems at their levels despite a negotiated multistep grievance procedure. Foremen might be instructed, for example, to "kick upstairs" all grievances, and stewards may be under directions to refer all matters to the shop committee.

Such practices inevitably will lead to more unresolved grievances at higher stages in the process. As the steel industry's Joint Study Committee on Grievance and Arbitration Procedure noted in its 1971 Report, the grievance procedure "can only function properly where full responsibility and authority is given to front line participants to investigate, review, screen, and resolve the everyday type of grievance."[2] Neither party is entirely comfortable with that arrangement. Management must put its welfare and interests in the hands of the ordinary foreman, and the union must give an individual steward the right to withdraw or settle a grievance—choices that may not be possible for one or both parties. Certainly giving authority to the lower-level representatives necessitates a significant training commitment. In any case, the procedures chosen for operating the grievance procedure can influence the level of grievance activity. Even more important than procedures, however, is the basic attitude of the parties toward resolving grievances. As Elkouri notes:

> The parties' attitude in handling grievances, probably more than in any other aspect of the labor-management relationship, indicates their good faith. Nowhere in that relationship is mutual good faith more important. The attitude of the parties is even more important than the type of grievance provisions contained in the agreement.... Moreover, a desire to settle grievances, rather than to win them, is essential.[3]

Even allowing for the great variation in grievance definitions that negotiated contract language and practice can produce, an alleged violation of the express terms of the collective bargaining agreement will always constitute a valid grievance. In most cases, such an allegation must be a formal complaint of wrongful or improper action under the contract. An allegation of contract violation may be formal or official, regardless of whether it is written or presented orally, but recognition that a complaint is a grievance by the union and by management is crucial to its status.

Certainly, all conceivable injustices are not grievable. It is a common misconception among employees that a valid grievance need only assert some connection with the notion of working conditions. Whether such a complaint is a valid grievance depends upon the terms of the collective bargaining agreement. Both management and the union have a legal obligation to administer the agreement as negotiated. Thus, in its most basic form, a valid grievance is an alleged breach, misinterpretation, or misapplication of the express terms of the contract.

Whether allegedly improper application of plant rules or regulations is also grievable depends upon the language of the contract and the practice of the parties. When such rules are actually negotiated as part of the contract, they are clearly grievable. Generally, rules of conduct, regulations, dress codes, etc., are considered related both to management rights and to terms and conditions of employment. Since collective bargaining requires the negotiation of wages, hours, and terms and conditions of employment, such issues usually are subject to the grievance procedure, at least regarding their application. However, management has the right to promulgate rules and regulations implementing its inherent right to manage—directing the work force, controlling facilities, scheduling and controlling production. Therefore, the actual making of rules and regulations may not be grievable.

Consider the following variations in grievance definition:

Example 1: A *grievance* is a formal allegation that the express terms of this Agreement have been violated.

Example 2: A *grievance* is an allegation or complaint that there has been a violation, misinterpretation, or improper application of the terms and conditions of this Agreement or any complaint alleging improper, arbitrary or discriminatory enforcement or application of rules, regulations, practices or procedures relating to wages, hours, and terms and conditions of employment.

Example 3: Any difference or dispute arising between the Union or any employee and the employer as to the meaning or application of this Agreement or as to wages, hours, and terms and conditions of employment, shall be subject to the grievance procedure.

Unless some other provision of the contract is directly violated, an allegation that management has no right to promulgate a particular plant rule may not be grievable at all under the language of example 1, especially if there is a strong management rights clause. Under the language of example 2, the promulgation of such a rule may not be grievable, but issues concerning its application probably would be. In the general language of example 3, which does not formally define a *grievance* at all, both the promulgation and the application of a rule may be grievable.

However, all relevant contract language, not just the grievance-arbitration section, must be examined in order to evaluate the contractual basis for a grievance. Suppose that a company agrees to the "reasonable" qualification that management rights be exercised "with sound judgment." Under such language, an arbitrator may be in the position of deciding not only whether the promulgation of a rule was within management's authority but also whether management exercised its authority "soundly." Such a limitation on management's rights undoubtedly will be tested by the union. The enormous effect of contract language on grievance interpretation is readily apparent.

As a general rule, certainly management has the right to promulgate rules. This right is qualified, as the Supreme Court noted in its *Fiberboard Paper Products Corp.* decision in 1964, by the principle that management must bargain over actions that materially affect terms and conditions of employment.[4] Further, the application of rules is a separate issue of contract administration that depends both on the definition of a grievance in the agreement and on other contract language. In most cases, even though an action may be clearly within management's rights, an allegation of arbitrary, capricious, discriminatory, inconsistent, or otherwise improper exercise of those rights will be grievable.

It is vitally important, then, for the parties to consider the implications of management's right to make and enforce reasonable rules at the time of negotiations and to indicate their intentions through contract language if possible. Regulations are frequently worded in terms more general than contract language in order to give supervisors discretion in enforcing them. If such regulations formally become a part of the agreement, management may find an arbitrator substituting his or her judgment for that of the supervisor in deciding whether a regulation was properly enforced. For the union, the issue is one of achieving degrees of control over the work place and over working conditions. Both the union and the employer would protect their interests best by developing acceptable contract language rather than by allowing their later actions to determine what is properly grievable as a contract violation.

PAST PRACTICE GRIEVANCES

In addition to charging a violation of contract language or its improper application, a grievance might validly allege a violation of standard or past practice. It is helpful to think about the issue of *practice* as comprising two separate but related categories of grievances. In the first category, the collective bargaining agreement is silent; the alleged practice is a working condition that could appropriately be termed an employee *benefit* that has become established through practice over time. Since the union and the employer are required by law to negotiate in good faith about terms and conditions of employment (working conditions), it is widely held by arbitrators that any favorable working conditions or benefits in place at the time of negotiations and not addressed specifically at the collective bargaining table are presumed in effect. Thus, if management intends some change to occur in working conditions, it must address that subject in negotiations since a change requires bargaining. Unilateral removal of a benefit is grievable and may also be an unfair labor practice, depending upon the circumstances.

This concept of past practice when the contract is silent arises because of the assumption that the parties may talk about any working conditions during negotiations and have the duty to bargain about them. Archibald Cox and John Dunlop argue that unless an intention to the contrary is clear, a collective bargaining agreement should be assumed "to carry forward for its term the major terms and conditions of employment, not covered by the agreement, which prevailed when the agreement was executed."[5] Such existing benefits and favorable conditions are silently recognized by negotiators when they form their demands in bargaining.[6] The Supreme Court recognized the importance of practice in the *Steelworkers Trilogy:*

> The labor arbitrator's source of law is not confined to the express provisions of the contract, as the industrial common law—the practices of the industry and the shop—is equally a part of the collective bargaining agreement though not expressed in it.[7]

The union will, properly, use the idea of practices as working conditions to expand the rights that it has protected under and through the contract. As one union leader training manual notes:

> The contract can also be expanded in another manner—one with which the [steward] may have little or no direct connection. This is the informal setting of working conditions without benefit of contract; when management doesn't object, they become work practices that may be considered as binding as a written contract provision.... The contract has been expanded by the men themselves in the age-old tradition of workers in combination—the forerunner of the union.[8]

That is not to say that management has no latitude whatever in the area of working conditions established by practice. It may still police those conditions against abuse, and the arrangements for their administration may change. Furthermore, it is conceivable that the underlying basis for an existing practice may change, thus making a change in the practice itself appropriate or necessary. For example, if a technological innovation in machinery changes the conditions that led to the original practice, the practice may be changed. Apart from these specific limitations, practices associated with working conditions or employee benefits may only be terminated with notice at the end of a contract so that they can become subject to future negotiations.

What must occur before such a practice can become established as a working condition and therefore be grievable? First, it must be an employee benefit or favorable condition. Second, the contract must be silent concerning the subject. Third, the practice must involve some significant frequency or duration; it cannot be a one-time benefit or condition. How much time is required varies with the factual circumstances. Fourth, the practice must be more than a simple gratuity.

If, for example, it has been a standard practice of an employer to provide a hot lunch over several years, or especially over several contracts, then a hot lunch may become an employee benefit that the employer may not terminate unilaterally, or perhaps even modify, even though lunches are not mentioned in the contract. Similarly, if a contract or plant rule specifies an 8-hour workday but the practice of the employer has been to permit employees to quit 10 minutes early to wash up, then wash-up time may become a practice if established with a significant frequency or duration. While the provision of a turkey or ham at Christmas may be a simple gratuity, if extended over several years or contracts the gift may become a practice and thereby a condition of employment.

If the union believes management has violated a practice, its obligation is to grieve in a timely fashion. Failure to do so may waive the right to have the practice continued since the absence of objection apparently indicates that the union believes management did not act improperly. Clearly a practice whose pattern is interrupted by a change will not meet the frequency and duration standard. The potential for practice grievances adds even more significance to the uniformity and consistency with which managers must implement the agreement and to the vigilance and vigor with which union representatives must enforce it.

Choosing to take the initiative in negotiating about existing working conditions may be counterproductive. Suppose that employees have been quitting work up to 10 minutes early for the past 5 years, over two agreements, to wash up. If neither the union nor the employer raises the issue of wash-up time at negotiations for the next contract, the union has a good chance of being able to protect the practice of wash-up time from unilateral change. Of course, this requires dealing with uncertainty—nowhere is it written that employees may quit 10 minutes early to wash up; they just do it, without objection from their supervisors. If the union, for whatever reason, tries to win a guarantee of wash-up time explicitly in the contract and does not succeed at the bargaining table, what it had gained through practice it might well lose. By making wash-up time an element in the bargain, the union is no longer entitled to argue that wash-up time is silently a part of the agreement. Similarly, if management attempts to negotiate into the agreement a particular method of operation and fails, it may lose the ability to claim that the procedure may be changed unilaterally as an exercise of management rights.

A second category of past practice arises when the contract is ambiguous rather than silent. In such a case, there is contract language but its meaning is not clear, or its normal meaning seems clear but its application to some new situation is not. When the language of the agreement is ambiguous, arbitrators frequently hold that the custom of the parties informs the meaning of the contract. Since each party has an obligation to administer the agreement properly and in good faith, ambiguities can be resolved in favor of the way in which the agreement is implemented, since any contrary course of action should provoke a grievance. Nevertheless, the practice being alleged must be specific and capable of clear description, not ambiguous simply because it arises from ambiguous language. Moreover, the union must be able to relate the practice clearly to the issue or contract clause being raised in the grievance. A practice "is not broader than the circumstances out of which it has arisen, although its scope can always be enlarged in the day-to-day administration of the agreement."9

What are the tests of the existence of a practice when the contract is ambiguous? First, the issue in question must neither be clearly a union prerogative nor a management right. Second, there must be substantial evidence of mutuality. Either by express or tacit agreement, the union and the employer must have allowed the practice to become established with significant frequency or over a substantial duration without objection. Third, the parties must take the action claimed to be a practice clearly and consistently each time the circumstances surrounding the practice arise. Fourth, the evidence must support the test of significant frequency or duration.

Frequently unions file grievances or management responds to grievances about past practice issues with an argument concerning intent; one or the other of the parties argues that its perspective on the ambiguous language is correct because of its intent at negotiations. The key component of practice is mutuality. In order to prevail with an argument concerning intent, the intent referred to must be shown to be mutual; it may not simply be a condition that occurred in the mind of one party at negotiations. Further, if practice has established the meaning of ambiguous contract language and the same language is continued in a new agreement, it is presumed to have the same meaning. Since the parties are totally free to raise new or old issues in negotiations, current conditions will prevail under the new contract unless discussions to the contrary occur.

Issues concerning practice are frequently quite complicated, involve difficult questions of evidence, and arise from differing perceptions of standard conduct or expected benefits. They therefore present particularly significant risks for both parties at arbitration. As Elkouri points out with respect to any arbitration, "the result reached in any given case may depend in part upon the thinking of the particular person who has been authorized by the parties to decide the case."[10] In addition, much depends on the accuracy and credibility of witness testimony and the skill of the advocates. Therefore, the parties are well advised to try to settle their own disputes concerning practice through the grievance procedure or negotiations rather than to let an arbitrator with less complete understanding of circumstances and implications make a decision for them that will be binding for the duration of the agreement. The only reliable protection against losing at arbitration is not arbitrating.

ALLEGATIONS OF ILLEGAL ACTIVITY

Allegations of illegal actions are usually not subject to the grievance procedure since courts or administrative agencies are the most directly appropriate forum. However, grievances alleging both a violation of the contract and a violation of the law are not uncommon. The interaction of the collective bargaining agreement and the law is not easily dismissed.

Since enunciating its *Spielberg Manufacturing Co.* decision in 1955, the National Labor Relations Board has reserved the option to defer to an arbitration award already issued when (1) the proceedings were fair and regular, (2) all parties agreed to be bound, (3) the decision was not repugnant to the purposes and policies of the federal law, and (4) the issue alleged to be an unfair labor practice was considered by the arbitrator.[11] Moreover, in *Collyer Insulated Wire* in 1971, the NLRB announced that it might decide in advance to defer to an arbitration not yet conducted if (1) the dispute arose within the confines of a long and productive relationship and there was no claim of enmity to employees' protected legal rights, (2) management has demonstrated its willingness to arbitrate disputes under a broad arbitration clause, and (3) the contract and its meaning lie at the center of the dispute.[12] In 1977 the NLRB modified its *Collyer* standards when it ruled in *General American Transportation Company* that it would not defer to arbitration in cases involving alleged discrimination against individuals.[13] Thus, the NLRB to date has drawn a distinction between collective and individual rights for possible deferral, but the board's policy has shifted considerably and may not be settled.

The interpretation of these standards is subject to a growing volume of case law, but the interaction of statutory violations and the grievance-arbitration procedure is quite complicated. Even given the *Spielberg* and *Collyer* decisions, the board has simply enunciated those conditions under which it *may* defer to arbitration. Therefore, charges of unfair labor practices could also be grievable and subject to settlement under a negotiated grievance-arbitration procedure, but the outcome of any particular dispute is largely dependent on the circumstances.

Many contracts contain an explicit recognition of the responsibility of the parties to obey all or certain relevant laws. Many agreements recognize a controlling influence of statutes such as those dealing with health and safety or equal employment opportunity. It is not unusual for the general language or concepts of the statute to be incorporated directly into contract language. In such instances, an alleged violation may be grievable as well as subject to legal action. However, even in these instances of overlapping language or concepts, the issue before an arbitrator will be specifically whether the contract, not the law, was violated. If an arbitrator were to issue an award that explicitly interpreted the law, the award may be very susceptible to being overturned on the grounds that the arbitrator exceeded his or her authority by going beyond the contract. On the other hand, if an arbitrator must choose between two interpretations, one consistent with the law and one inconsistent, he or she might properly choose the former, thereby using the law for the purpose of accurately interpreting the contract.

When the language or standards of a statute, as well as reference to its authority, become part of the agreement, disputes can become exceedingly complex. Suppose that a union and management agree to be bound by the provisions of the Equal Pay Act, among other equal employment opportunity statutes, and agree specifically that, in the language of the statute, there will be no discrimination on the basis of sex "for equal work on jobs the performance of which requires equal skill, effort and responsibility, and which are performed under similar working conditions."[14] Since passage of the act in 1963, a large volume of case law that holds that the jobs being compared need not be identical but must be "substantially equal," has developed. Numerous cases illustrate the application of a "substantially equal" standard in the interpretation of the statute. In filing a grievance alleging unequal pay because of sex under this contract language, should a union develop its arguments according to the legal concepts that have evolved? Should an employer respond to a grievance using these concepts? Should an arbitrator apply the concepts in resolving the dispute? Such questions raise largely unresolved problems and usually can be answered only on a case-by-case basis.

Collective bargaining agreements can provide, with complete legitimacy, that employees who choose to exercise certain statutory rights through legal proceedings lose the opportunity that they would otherwise have to grieve the same issue. A contract might stipulate that an employee may not grieve an alleged act of discrimination if he or she chooses to take the matter to court or to an administrative agency. Furthermore, some public sector agreements provide that an employee who wishes to dispute an adverse personnel action may choose either the older civil service procedure for appeals or the contractual grievance procedure but may not use both channels.

An individual employee who believes that his or her legal rights have been violated usually retains access to the courts regardless of the access to or outcome from a grievance-arbitration procedure. If the contract provides that a given issue is grievable, an employee has two arenas in which to seek relief and gets "two bites of the apple." As the Supreme Court ruled in *Alexander* v. *Gardner-Denver* in 1974, statutory and contractual rights have separate foundations, one in law and the other in the collective bargaining agreement.[15] Accordingly, the outcome of a grievance alleging discrimination will not be binding upon a court hearing the same dispute as a suit under Title VII. Although the court may give appropriate weight to the arbitrator's award, it must hear the case *de novo* and is not bound by the award.

In some instances, public sector employees may have additional legal rights that private sector employees do not enjoy. For example, personnel actions taken by a public employer are arguably government action and subject to constitutional guarantees of citizenship rights. The Constitution prohibits only governments from interference with individual liberties and does not address relationships between private individuals. A private sector employee may not be able to assert successfully the right to free speech in either a grievance or a lawsuit. But a public sector employee may be able both to sue and, depending upon the language of the contract, to grieve an alleged breach of that right.

Even if an agreement does not explicitly commit the parties to obey a particular law, some arbitrators hold that obeying the law is basic to the collective bargaining relationship; therefore, an alleged illegal action violating the spirit of the agreement must be subject to the grievance procedure. But far more arbitrators assert the traditional view that the arbitrator is restricted to the interpretation of the contract and must leave legal analysis to the courts. Certainly few arbitrators would interpret an agreement in such a way as to direct a party to disobey a law. The problem of overlapping legal and contractual considerations is not new; a grievance about proper overtime payment in 1939 could have raised a contractual issue as well as legal questions under the Fair Labor Standards Act. But there is no doubt that the great acceleration in legislation affecting the employment relationship since 1960 has increased the complexity and significance of the problem. As more and more states pass statutes concerning employee privacy and access to personnel files or consider legally guaranteed due process in discipline cases, the dilemmas for arbitrators and for the parties will increase.

Little practical guidance can be given to the parties with respect to the development of grievance and arbitration cases that raise both legal and contractual issues. Certainly no skilled advocate will ignore arguments grounded in the law if they are supportive. Much will depend upon the language of the contract, the presentation of the case, and the disposition of the arbitrator. To the extent such mixed cases are complex, their outcome is increasingly uncertain at arbitration; the parties would be well advised to seek diligently the grounds for some compromise settlement.

It is not unusual for an employee to feel that he or she has been treated unfairly in some respect. If the alleged unfair treatment involves a disciplinary action, the employee can grieve management's failure to show just cause. What happens if discipline is not involved? Suppose that one supervisor permits employees to bring in radios during the World Series but another does not. Clearly whatever rights, duties, and responsibilities are conferred generally upon individual employees are conferred equally unless the agreement specifies otherwise. Yet this does not imply that an absolute equality must prevail in the way that employees are treated by supervisors or other managers. It is impractical and impossible to expect that all supervisors will treat all employees with complete equality or that the same considerations will be relevant to all employees regardless of responsibility or work site. Thus, a complaint or a grievance alleging unfair treatment, other than discipline, may be processed, but the union could have great difficulty finding a contractual basis for it. Such a grievance may be impossible to sustain at arbitration, no matter how "fair" the relief sought.

Conceivably some management action could treat an individual employee or group so outrageously that an arbitrator would attempt to apply some standard of equity. Hopefully, most instances of such treatment would be settled in the grievance procedure before arbitration. Arbitrators are exceedingly reluctant to stray outside the "four corners of the contract"; clearly the arbitrator's role is not to dispense a personal version of industrial justice. Yet many agreements contain a preamble or some other section witnessing the intent of the parties to ensure fair treatment or expressing some similar joint intention of good faith. Such language might be enough to include in the process a grievance alleging unfair treatment. Whether an issue of unfair treatment can be validly grieved usually will depend on the degree to which contract language supplies some support and perhaps on the degree of the alleged unfairness.

Far more importantly, however, the parties have a mechanism to deal with the perceived problem and to resolve it without resort to technicalities. With all employee complaints, little contribution will be made to a stable collective bargaining relationship by overly legalistic treatment of complaints by either party. The union inherits only trouble from a dissatisfied employee whom it cannot help; management cannot benefit from the loss of morale and perhaps also production or quality that results from unresolved disputes. Since employee complaints of unfair treatment frequently have no practicable remedy regardless of their status as grievances, the therapeutic value of hearing a complaint and responding directly to it by using the early steps of procedure may be of great usefulness to both parties.

Should management be able to file grievances against the union? There is nothing to prevent an agreement that both parties have access to the grievance-arbitration procedure; while not frequent, such arrangements are not unusual. In the majority of contracts, however, only the union or an employee can grieve. This is consistent with the usual view that management has the role of implementing the agreement, and the union, the role of enforcing it. Further, since management generally is viewed as the acting party, allowing only the union to have access to the procedure reinforces the notion that management does not need to file grievances because it always has the option of changing its actions. Some employers insist, however, that as a matter of fairness, management ought to be able to hold the union accountable for living up to the agreement since the legal obligation is shared equally.

Most employers do not take such a position. Section 301 of the Taft-Hartley Labor-Management Relations Act guarantees the employer the right to sue a union for breach of contract in the event of a strike when a no-strike agreement is in effect. This is usually what most employers want to hold the union accountable for; most find the legal protection not only sufficient but also much more desirable than the ability to grieve against the union. If a grievance-arbitration clause stipulated the grievance procedure as the method for resolving all disputes and gave management equal access to it, conceivably management could have its flexibility severely limited by being ordered to arbitrate certain issues rather than being able to sue. Arbitration may yield a final decision more quickly, but it is unlikely to yield the kind of damages for breach of contract that an employer could win in a more time-consuming suit. Securing an injunction to curtail a strike in violation of a no-strike clause is relatively easy and speedy. Most employers, therefore, prefer the traditional role of acting and leave it to the union to grieve if it believes that the agreement is not being properly implemented.

Reference Notes

[1]*Boys Markets Inc.* v. *Retail Clerks, Local 770,* 398 U.S. 235 (1970).
[2]Coordinating Committee, Steel Companies and United Steelworkers of America, "Report of the Joint Study Committee on Grievance and Arbitration Procedure," June 14, 1971, 11.
[3]Frank Elkouri and Edna Asper Elkouri, *How Arbitration Works,* 3rd. ed. (Washington, D.C.: Bureau of National Affairs), 1973, 110.
[4]*Fibreboard Paper Products Corp.* v. *NLRB,* 379 U.S. 203 (1964).
[5]Archibald Cox and John Dunlop, "The Duty to Bargain Collectively During the Term of an Existing Agreement," *Harvard Law Review* 63 (1950), 1116-1117 (as quoted in Elkouri, *How Arbitration Works,* 393).

[6]Elkouri, *How Arbitration Works*, 398-399.

[7]*United Steelworkers of America* v. *Warrior & Gulf Navigation Co.*, 363 U.S. 574 (1960).

[8]Duane Beeler and Harry Kurshenbaum, *Roles of the Labor Leader* (Chicago: Union Representative, 1969), 23.

[9]Richard Mittenthal as quoted in Elkouri, *How Arbitration Works*, 392.

[10]Elkouri, *How Arbitration Works*, 391.

[11]*Spielberg Manufacturing Company*, 112 NLRB 1080 (1955).

[12]*Collyer Insulated Wire*, 192 NLRB 837 (1971).

[13]*General American Transportation Company*, 228 NLRB 2 (1977).

[14]29 USC §206 (d) (1).

[15]*Alexander* v. *Gardner-Denver Co.*, 415 U.S. 36 (1974).

CHAPTER 3

Elements of the Grievance Procedure

Most negotiated grievance procedures are similar in basic structure, even though they vary in the number of steps. Typically, grievance procedures begin with an initial step, during which grievances can be investigated and possibly resolved informally, and proceed to later formal steps, during which written records are kept and firm positions are developed. At each higher step, the representatives of the parties are individuals with greater responsibility for influencing or making policy decisions within their organizations. The further a case moves in the procedure, the more remote become the facts, evidence, and individuals involved in the actual incident or action. However, the likelihood of resolution may increase for some cases precisely because the vested interests and firm positions of those persons immediately concerned are more remote. Following the steps within the employer's organization, some form of binding arbitration by a neutral is the last step.

The level at which a particular grievance is most susceptible to settlement, assuming that the parties genuinely seek a resolution, is largely a function of the complexity of the issue and its importance to their basic interests. Clearly the grievance procedure works most effectively if the attitude of the employer and the union favors settlement, without a sacrifice of fundamental interests, rather than merely "winning." In order for this attitude to be translated into constructive action, the representatives involved at each step must have the authority to settle grievances within their sphere of general responsibility. Further, the parties must endeavor jointly to resolve grievances at the lowest level appropriate to any given issue. Figure 3-1 illustrates the structure of a model grievance procedure.

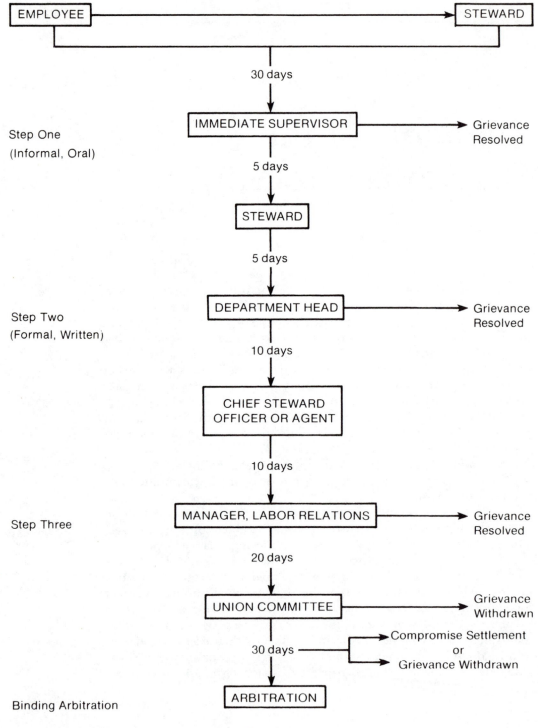

FIGURE 3-1
Model Grievance Procedure

EMPLOYEE — STEWARD

30 days

Step One
(Informal, Oral)

IMMEDIATE SUPERVISOR → Grievance Resolved

5 days

STEWARD

5 days

Step Two
(Formal, Written)

DEPARTMENT HEAD → Grievance Resolved

10 days

CHIEF STEWARD
OFFICER OR AGENT

10 days

Step Three

MANAGER, LABOR RELATIONS → Grievance Resolved

20 days

UNION COMMITTEE → Grievance Withdrawn

30 days → Compromise Settlement
or
Grievance Withdrawn

Binding Arbitration

ARBITRATION

In the model, time limits are specified for each step. Those illustrated are only suggestive of the relationships among the various steps; there are no standard time limits, and actual practices vary widely. Many, but by no means all, contracts stipulate the length of time for an employee to initiate a grievance after he or she first knows, or should know, about the circumstances initiating the complaint. Usually this initial time period begins when management takes some action, such as official notification of a new rule or formal notice of a personnel action such as promotion, transfer, furlough, or discipline.

Generally management must have taken the action before a grievance can allege validly that the agreement was violated. An employee can't grieve on the basis of suspicion that he or she is about to be disciplined improperly. There are some exceptions. A union with evidence that the employer is beginning the process of contracting out work in violation of the agreement need not wait until the contractual arrangements have been finalized before grieving. When an employee or union believes that management is about to take some action that violates the agreement, communicating promptly an official notice to that effect usually will lead to the necessary confrontation without raising technical questions about whether an actual grievance is appropriate. The initial time limit helps to ensure that real problems will not be left to fester by requiring that an employee or union present a grievance in a timely manner or lose the right to have it considered. A failure to present a grievance within the initial time limit can be a reason for dismissal of the grievance, regardless of merit. Failure to advance a grievance to the next step within the stipulated time limit usually results in the disposition of the grievance according to management's response at the prior step.

Nearly all contracts stipulate time limits after each step during which management must respond to the grievance. If the union finds this response unsatisfactory, it must present the grievance at the next higher step within specified time limits. The time limits between the steps promote prompt and efficient processing and prevent either party from abusing the procedure by deliberate delay. The employer's interest in time limits follows from the need to promote efficient production by identifying and resolving problems as quickly as possible. The union's interest is much more closely related to its function of protecting employee rights since, assuming that a no-strike clause is in the agreement, the work will continue as directed by management while the grievance is being processed. Management is under no expectation or requirement to suspend the action in question while the issue is being decided. Ultimately, if the union is unsatisfied with management's response at the last internal step and the union is unwilling to withdraw the grievance or simply let it die, the union must notify the employer of its demand for third-party arbitration within the time limits specified.

A few contracts provide that management's failure to respond within time limits will result in the grievance being sustained. In most cases, however, a failure by management to respond within the time limits permits the union to advance the grievance immediately to the next higher step.

THE GRIEVANCE PROCEDURE
AS NEGOTIATION

The grievance procedure is an extension of the negotiation process in several respects. First, the "adjustment" of grievances is included in the concept of collective bargaining in the National Labor Relations Act, which anticipates that questions arising under collective agreements will be negotiated. The legal duty to bargain in good faith does not terminate with the ratification of an agreement and continues not only into the negotiation of successor agreements but also into the resolution of disputes under the current contract. Second, the grievance procedure is an extension of negotiation because the parties use it to clarify ambiguous contract language and to ensure implementation of the agreement according to their collective intentions. Third, both the employer and the union will certainly examine the history of grievances under a current agreement in assessing the need for new or revised contract language under a successor agreement to be negotiated. Collective bargaining, then, is a continuous process, of which the grievance procedure is a fundamental part. As the Supreme Court noted in *Warrior & Gulf Navigation Co.*, one of the *Trilogy* cases:

> Apart from matters that the parties specifically exclude, all of the questions on which the parties disagree must therefore come within the scope of the grievance and arbitration provisions of the collective agreement. The grievance procedure is, in other words, a part of the continuous collective bargaining process.[1]

Negotiating grievance settlements, which may involve compromises in the relief being sought, is not inconsistent with the requirement that each grievance be processed on its own merits. This is the union's obligation under its duty of fair representation. Any apparent inconsistency is simply a reflection of the uncertainty and ambiguity inherent in the process of bargaining and the process of balancing collective and individual rights and obligations. Horse-trading of grievances, in which large numbers are withdrawn in exchange for others that are settled, is uniformly condemned if carried out without respect to the merits of the individual disputes. This is not to say that horse-trading does not occur; to the contrary, it occurs frequently. But a union that settles grievances without respect to merit runs a considerable risk of breaching its duty of fair representation. (The problems of merit review of grievances by the union are discussed later in this chapter.)

How does a union navigate the narrow passage between too willingly compromising grievances and championing each one according to its merit on the other? Duane Beeler, in his union training manual, *Roles of the Labor Leader,* describes the issue:

> Chaos would result in the administration of the contract if the union followed any policy except that of handling each grievance on its own merit. And yet, even though horsetrading is a bad term and all manuals deplore the procedure, there *is* a process of accommodation that allows both sides to maneuver in grey areas on problems that do not permit legal solutions. However, these grey areas never involve contract application or labor-management policies.[2]

Grievances involving contract application or the labor-management relationship should not be horse-traded for important reasons. The employer, except under the most extraordinary circumstances, has no interest in limiting its discretion any further than the contract already mandates. Since management has virtually all rights in the absence of collective bargaining, the agreement itself is a significant limitation, and management constantly will direct its efforts toward ensuring that its remaining discretionary authority is not compromised. The union, in order to meet its duty of fair representation, must vigorously and consistently enforce unambiguous contract language and also must present a consistent interpretation of ambiguous language.

Still, there is a wide variety of what might be termed *everyday* grievances, involving different sorts of employee complaints or disagreements over proper procedure, which provide ample room for negotiated settlements. Even with the most rigorous attempts at specificity, most agreements contain a significant amount of ambiguous language as well as provisions describing actions or procedures that involve discretion and judgment. For example, despite years of experience and volumes of arbitral opinion defining and applying *just cause* as a disciplinary concept, the standard remains highly ambiguous when applied to the factual circumstances of particular cases. Similarly, a provision requiring seniority to govern promotions "if ability is relatively equal" leaves room for valid compromise in at least some factual situations.

As Beeler describes the gray area where the parties have room to maneuver and negotiate, many grievances are relatively weak in their contractual base but relatively strong on equity considerations. In those instances, several valid resolutions are plausible. First, the union might simply withdraw the grievance or let it die. Without a strong contractual base, the union would have a difficult time prevailing at arbitration, especially if the agreement defines a grievance narrowly as an alleged violation of the express terms of the contract. Second, the company might allow the grievance on a nonprecedential basis, recognizing the equity argument, if the union agrees to drop some other equally weak or weaker case. Finally, the parties may be able to reach a compromise settlement. The union might accept less than the relief initially sought, perhaps a reduction in discipline rather than a total retraction, with management retaining at least some of its action and the legitimacy of its rationale.[3]

In virtually all grievance settlements, both parties probably will want to stipulate that the compromise is without prejudice to their respective positions and that it is nonprecedential in future cases. Moreover, most arbitrators consider it to be at least in bad form, if not patently improper, for one party to introduce evidence about an offered compromise in order to demonstrate that the other party believes its own case to be weak. As sophisticated labor relations professionals, arbitrators recognize that negotiation involves taking positions with which one may not fully agree in order to test the degree of maneuverability with the other party.

A clear view of the union's rights, duties, and obligations in negotiating grievance settlements is important. Whereas management's interests are relatively straightforward, many managers and many union members do not understand the delicacy of the union's position. While a bargaining unit member is entitled to rigorous union enforcement of rights won in collective bargaining, an employee is not entitled to union enforcement of his or her own interpretation of a particular contract clause or support for his or her own sense of fairness. The touchstone for the union is its duty to enforce the contract, whatever the implications for individual bargaining unit members or, for that matter, for management. As a party to the agreement, the union, not individual members, incurs this legal responsibility.

It may well be that protecting the interests of an individual or group does not best serve the interests of the entire bargaining unit. Thus, the union is fully empowered to reach a compromise settlement of a grievance even though the settlement is contrary to the wishes of one or several of the employees affected as long as the settlement does not violate the agreement. Nevertheless, the political problems inherent in the balancing of individual and collective rights within the union as an organization cannot be minimized. Even though legally permissible, it may be politically impossible for the union to refuse to file or carry forward a grievance that has limited merit but affects an important individual or significant group. Likewise, a compromise settlement may be impossible, practically, for the union to accept if a significant individual or an important group within the rank and file is adamantly opposed.

Despite all the political difficulties, there are three major reasons why the union should seek to negotiate grievance settlements if possible. First, the ability to settle problems increases the respect and power of the union within the labor-management relationship. In the landmark case of *Vaca* v. *Sipes* (1967), in which the Supreme Court most clearly set forth the arbitrary, discriminatory, and bad faith tests for the union's fair representation duty, the court lauded efforts to negotiate grievance settlements according to the merits of the grievance. The negotiation process strengthens the relationship between union and employer because each must compromise to reach a solution, a process that builds trust and respect. In the view of the Supreme Court, the process of negotiating grievances generates pressure for treating similar problems consistently and thus helps to isolate, and perhaps resolve, major problem areas of contract interpretation, "thereby enhancing the union's interest as bargaining agent."[4]

Second, as Beeler points out, negotiating grievance settlements actually may be a way for the union to increase the rights and benefits of bargaining unit members beyond those specifically enumerated in the contract. In a strong labor-management relationship, compromise in the grievance process may lead to settlements on some grievances that would otherwise be lost because of weaknesses in their contractual underpinnings. "The basic idea," as Beeler expresses it, "is to handle the best cases, and let these gains flow to the weaker cases."[5] To be sure, this process does not occur in secret; management is entirely aware of the union's objectives. But there are many instances in which management might be willing to grant certain grievances as the result of negotiations in exchange for solutions to other problems that it considers more serious or simply in order to remove frustrating thorns in its side.

The third reason why it is in the union's interests to seek compromise settlements is that the alternative, demanding arbitration, entails substantial risks, a reason that applies in equal measure to management.

> Arbitration can be a form of Russian roulette, with the party who presents a case rarely knowing how he will come out.
> Preferable is a negotiated settlement of grievances, with both parties protecting their vital interests, through a process of compromise and accomodation.[6]

Arbitration provides final resolution for disputes that the parties have failed to settle themselves. Even if the union could afford the cost of taking to arbitration each grievance rejected by management at the last step in the procedure, it would not want to take them all. Even though management is able to force the union to decide whether to arbitrate on all grievances simply by rejecting them, it would not want to risk arbitration of certain issues. An arbitrator's award interprets that section of the agreement for the duration of the contract. In many instances, the flexibility that comes with uncertainty about the application of particular contract language may be far preferable to the finality that comes with an arbitrator's award. Although the losing party can always seek to renegotiate favorable language in that section of the next contract, it must then bargain for the change, assuming that it is possible to achieve.

In some cases, a victory at arbitration would be sweet, but a loss would be disastrous. In other cases, a victory might be advantageous in some circumstances or for some people, but disadvantageous in other circumstances or for more people. In still other instances, arbitrating a particularly sensitive issue might adversely affect the labor-management relationship in such a way that settlement is preferable from the standpoint of long-range interests. These disincentives to arbitration are inherent; negotiation is the preferred manner of grievance resolution according to the law and to the realities of the collective bargaining process. Thus, grievance resolution need not be motivated by good hearts or by rational decisions to seek fully "mature," "productive," or "positive" labor-management relationships. Such motivations may be difficult to identify in the real world. But there are ample reasons related directly to the selfish best interest of the parties to suggest that using the grievance procedure to resolve problems between the union and management makes sense.

THE INFORMAL STEP

In some contracts, the informal, oral presentation of a complaint to the immediate supervisor constitutes the first official step in the grievance procedure. In others, the informal stage precedes the first official step, which occurs only after the complaint has been reduced to writing. Regardless of which model is used, the informal step usually involves the immediate supervisor or the manager at the lowest level with authority to settle the complaint and the employee, with or without a steward. Sometimes, however, the steward alone presents the complaint as the representative of the employee.

The chief functions of the initial stage of the grievance procedure are confrontation and fact finding; a dispute is joined when the employee or steward and the supervisor come face to face to identify, to discuss, and hopefully to resolve a problem. Prior to the confrontation, the parties may not even realize that a problem exists, much less appreciate its dimensions. Confrontation and fact finding at the initial step also help to separate *complaints* from *grievances*. Because a complaint must be subjected at least to preliminary investigation at the informal step in order for it to be discussed, the first stage of the grievance procedure also provides a valuable opportunity for reconnaissance of the other party's view of the issue. In the process of investigating and discussing the complaint at the earliest confrontation point, an opportunity arises for evaluating the strength of the other party's viewpoint should a difference of opinion remain.

A perceptive steward may be able to test several alternative arguments in the course of an informal discussion in order to assess management's possible responses, at least at the level of the supervisor. If the actions of the supervisor are directly at issue, the steward may be able to test the strength of the supervisor's ability to justify them. Likewise, a perceptive supervisor may be able to assess the seriousness of the complaint and the likelihood of the union's strong support. If the employee's actions are directly at issue, the supervisor may be able to assess the employee's ability to defend against a management accusation. If the informal discussion reveals alternative acceptable actions or some misunderstanding or misinterpretation of events or intentions, the issue might be settled on the spot. On the other hand, if the discussion indicates that the complaint will likely become a grievance and proceed to the first formal step, each party should be better equipped to determine what evidence and arguments will be required for presenting the strongest possible case. Should the supervisor decide that the complaint is justified, acting promptly to resolve it will usually enhance respect and therefore effectiveness. The supervisor who delays needlessly or acts only begrudgingly when an employee clearly has a valid complaint will only cause a lack of respect from others.

Even if one or both of the first step representatives realize that the complaint would fail as a grievance, the employee or steward should still present it and the supervisor should still hear it. The processes of confrontation and fact finding are therapeutic regardless of the outcome. The informal step is a valuable opportunity for letting off steam when employees have emotional complaints but not valid grievances. A trained steward knows that a responsible supervisor must reject an unfounded complaint but may be able to turn that realization to the union's advantage. Even though the complaint surely will be rejected, the union gets the opportunity to help a member and also benefits from a process that allows an emotional employee, who is going to lose, to let off steam. A trained supervisor will appreciate the dynamics of this process and allow it to occur; the employee later will be less emotional and the supervisor will have an opportunity to be fair but firm. Although the need for this kind of human relations training for both stewards and supervisors is recognized almost universally, trained and perceptive stewards and supervisors are rare; most first-step grievance meetings are at best a sham and at worst counterproductive to effective labor relations. But the objectives of such training and the benefits that it brings are no less important or desirable.

Purely from the standpoint of selfish interests, the parties benefit from effective first-step grievance meetings. Unless the complaint is outrageous or lacks all merit and has no contractual basis, the union has little to gain by explaining to a member why it cannot help. The employee inevitably will demand to know just what he or she is paying dues for and the well-intentioned, "responsible" explanation will probably result in hard feelings, if not internal political problems. Thus, there is much natural pressure for the steward's assisting the employee in making the complaint if it has at least some merit and leaving the onus on the supervisor to reject it. Since grievances are informal at the initial step, the union has little stake in the outcome at that point. There is also little practical choice for the supervisor. Taking a legalistic stance by refusing to deal with the complaint because it has no contractual basis will only generate hard feelings against the supervisor personally and management in general. Moreover, a consistent refusal to deal with complaints because they may not be valid grievances may lead to the union's using the grievance machinery to persuade higher management that the supervisor is incapable of dealing openly and honestly with employees. The union will have an easy time inundating the supervisor with complaints and grievances if that becomes a deliberate objective. First-line supervision is an awesomely difficult job; few do it well and most who do advance to higher levels. Maintaining productivity and quality standards for extended periods are impossible unless the supervisor deals openly and honestly with grievances at the first step.

Natural pressures exist for formalizing even the first step, but if the agreement provides for an informal initial stage, it is greatly in the interest of the parties to maintain informality. Stewards may be inclined to write out complaints because they believe that they can be more effective in writing or because a written complaint seems more demonstrative of the union's activity on behalf of the member. However, a written complaint actually may prevent or sidetrack the inevitable confrontation. Rather than dissipating emotion, written records tend to justify, formalize, and preserve it; they nearly always tend to make positions more rigid. Supervisors, too, may want to write out a response in the interest of clarity or, more likely, in order to justify personal actions for the record. Even more importantly, generating a written record at the informal step opens the door for a variety of possible errors that can compromise positions later in the grievance procedure. The steward may write a factual inaccuracy that will be difficult to explain or correct without at least a loss of negotiating power. The supervisor may commit management to a particular view or course of action that is not in its interests or inconsistent with actions in similar situations. Finally, the therapeutic value of open, informal confrontation and fact finding is lost if the first step in the grievance procedure is formalized.

Properly used, the informal step of the grievance procedure can be a mechanism for settling everyday disputes amicably, for separating complaints from grievances, for identifying significant problems that may become serious grievances, for generating the facts relevant to grievance issues, and for reconnoitering the potential strategy of the other party. By encouraging confrontation and fact finding, the informal step facilitates open communication between individual employees, the union, and management at the lowest level. If the representatives of the parties are perceptive and trained in human relations and contract administration skills, the informal step of the grievance procedure can be enormously valuable in the development of a constructive labor-management relationship.

UNREPRESENTED EMPLOYEES

What should a supervisor do if approached directly by an employee with a grievance in the absence of a union steward or, more to the point, by an employee who is adamant about not involving the union? Section 9 (a) of the National Labor Relations Act stipulates that the union is the exclusive representative of all members of the bargaining unit for purposes of collective bargaining, which is defined in section 8 (d) to include negotiation of any question arising under a collective bargaining agreement. However, section 9 (a) includes the following proviso:

> [A]ny individual employee or a group of employees shall have the right at any time to present grievances to their employer and to have such grievances adjusted, without the intervention of the bargaining representative, as long as the adjustment is not inconsistent with the terms of a collective bargaining contract or agreement then in effect: *Provided further,* That the bargaining representative has been given opportunity to be present at such adjustment.[7]

The safest interpretation, therefore, is that if the supervisor does intend to "adjust" the complaint or grievance, the union should at least be informed. Further, if such adjustment is to be accomplished in a meeting, the union should be given an opportunity to be present, although it has no right to intervene.

Most supervisors are well aware that, from the union's point of view, adjustments to employee complaints or grievances that do not affect wages, hours, or other terms and conditions of employment are virtually inconceivable. In most circumstances, the union will want to have its representative present at meetings concerning employee grievances because of the union's central objective and obligation of protecting employee rights. Besides, if the complaint has no merit and involves no contractual violation, the presence of a steward may permit the union to share some of the "blame," in the employee's eyes, for the rejection. For similar reasons, many supervisors make it a practice always to involve stewards when they warn or discipline employees. The supervisor secures a witness from the opposing party and, more importantly, sets in motion a kind of peer pressure dynamic in which the union representative, from a sense of obligation, probably will reinforce to the employee the implications of the warning.

Why should the union want to be involved, even in everyday complaints, rather than simply encouraging employees to take up the issues directly with their supervisors? The latter course would avoid the risk of seeming to be "in bed" with management at times and would also conserve stewards' time and energy for more significant grievances. Besides, many employees would prefer that the union not be involved, believing that the personal touch is essential for settling disputes and that the union representative will provoke an adversarial response. Moreover, some employees fear that a troublemaker label will be attached to them if they involve the union in a complaint or grievance.

One primary reason why the union usually will work tirelessly to be involved in all employee complaints or grievances is that its function is to protect employee rights, individually and collectively. The best-equipped individual to fulfill that role is probably the union's grievance representative, who should know, or will have access to, knowledge about the contract, relevant laws, past practices, and the rules and regulations governing working conditions at the employment site. Few individual employees have that knowledge, even though they may vigorously base their arguments on "the law" or the contract, because the individual employee ordinarily has no need for that information. Such knowledge can be crucially important even to everyday complaints. In reality, for a variety of reasons that stretch from insufficient budget to negligence to simple ignorance, many stewards are untrained, inept, and inarticulate in handling grievances. For that matter, so are many supervisors. But, assuming that the parties have provided their representatives with appropriate training, the steward is in the best position to protect employee rights.

Further, many people overestimate the effectiveness of the personal touch or their own ability to confront a supervisor forthrightly with a complaint. From the union's point of view, the simple presence of a steward can ensure that no intimidation, real or imagined, occurs. Employees often tend to misunderstand management's attitude toward the filing of grievances. It is a natural tendency not to want complaints and problems; sometimes a lack of complaints is viewed as an indicator of good performance. But a competent manager knows that working with people inevitably will involve some problems and differences in judgment or opinion and will not be threatened by grievances. If the disputes are sincere and the confrontations are direct and open, management has little cause for viewing employees who file grievances as troublemakers. To the extent that supervisors might have such attitudes, they are likely to carry over into all forms of complaint and, from the union's perspective, it is the employee's best protection if retaliation does occur.

A more important reason why the union probably will insist on involvement even with individual complaints is that, in any work group, there are few isolated, entirely individual complaints. Virtually every dispute, whether or not it involves terms and conditions of employment, affects other employees individually or in groups. Almost any supervisor's response to a complaint or grievance will have implications for other employees in the same circumstances, for the union, and for management:

> To the steward, the simple grievance is never simple; it almost always has overtones within the department. If the grievance doesn't affect the work situation, it may well affect the social relationships... in the group. A case that may seem good for an individual worker may upset the relationships....[8]

For these same reasons, there are also few simple grievances from the perspective of the first-level supervisor, whose primary responsibility is to maintain a high level of production within the work group.

The most fundamental reason why the union views its role in processing grievances as critically important follows from its status as the legal coequal of the employer in the administration of the contract. Once a contract is negotiated, the grievance procedure gives employees a voice in determining day-to-day working conditions. But rights are secured only when consistently and appropriately exercised; the union as the exclusive representative has a vested interest in participating in the resolution of complaints and grievances. Especially in view of timeliness standards, the union must try to contain complaints and grievances within the grievance procedure, which it controls, in order to police the implementation of the agreement vigilantly and vigorously. Any management would object if a union suddenly challenged a practice after knowingly permitting it to exist for an extended period. Management rightfully would question why the union didn't raise an objection at the earliest opportunity if it believed that management was not acting properly. But even the most well-organized steward system cannot be aware of all potential or arguable contractual violations unless individual employees come forward with them. Without a detailed knowledge of day-to-day problems, union representatives will not be in an effective position either to enforce the current agreement or to seek necessary changes in the contract at future negotiations.

THE FORMAL STEPS

Specific suggestions for processing grievances in the formal steps of the grievance procedure are provided in Chapter 4. In general, the primary function of the formal steps is to narrow the scope of the dispute to the specific issue of disagreement between the union and the employer. This narrowing occurs because the formal steps require even more complete investigation of the facts and evidence bearing on the case by both parties; as a result, their positions are likely to become more and more rigid as the grievance proceeds to higher steps. In the course of accumulating evidence and marshaling arguments, each party develops a comprehensive version of the facts as they support its contractual argument—a theory of the case. Hopefully, the result of narrowing the issue in dispute at each successive step will be that the parties achieve a clear view of the possibilities for and costs involved in settlement and, ultimately, of the risks in allowing the issue to be decided in arbitration. As the case advances through the grievance steps, each party's assessment of its winability at arbitration should influence the degree to which it is willing to consider compromise settlements.

The formal steps are also the appropriate place for complete consultation by the respective representatives with other appropriate individuals in their organizations. The union representative should apprise the grievance committee or union officers of the grievance no later than the point when it is formalized. If necessary, members of the negotiating team might be consulted and the perspective of the international may be sought. Consultation is of paramount importance for management representatives. To a far greater degree than their union counterparts, they have the authority to commit the employer to a course of action through their decisions. Especially when a complaint requires contractual interpretation for a response, the management representative must consult closely with superiors as well as with industrial or employee relations personnel no later than the point when the grievance becomes formalized. Through this consultation, the management representative will learn management's philosophical view of the issue, the negotiation history, and any other information important to the case. Only by requiring consultation with those in policy-making and coordinating positions can management avoid the establishment of unfavorable practices through inconsistent contract administration by individual supervisors. Further, the union's written grievance and management's written response at each step in the procedure become the official record of the case. Consultation prior to the development of the written record is crucial because of the difficulty of later undoing the damage that may result from a poorly written grievance or management response.

Union procedures for handling formal grievances vary greatly. Employees may be responsible for presenting complaints to their immediate supervisors with union assistance, but the union may be responsible for writing official grievances and arguing the case at all formal steps. Employees may have the entire responsibility of writing and arguing grievances, but with union assistance. In still other instances, the employee writes the grievance but the union argues it at grievance meetings, perhaps with a right to modify what the employee has written. In still other instances, the union may both write and argue all grievances on the employee's behalf.

Management too has choices in handling grievances. Management must decide how much authority to give representatives at the lower formal steps to resolve grievances. Will the managers who receive written grievances be able, on their own authority, to investigate the issues and write responses? Will supervisors be directed to refer all grievances to industrial relations personnel, who will participate in all meetings as management's spokesperson and write all responses? The choices have implications for the functioning of the grievance procedure, the effectiveness of communication within management channels, and the degree to which labor relations training will be required of grievance representatives.

In instances where the union allows or encourages individual employees to file grievances independently, it has little control over the grievance procedure, at least in the early steps. Employees can be inarticulate in framing the issue and describing appropriate relief. Especially if the union cannot modify the grievance after it is filed, either by contract or by practice of the parties, sacrificing control over the grievance procedure can produce serious obstacles to the union's effectiveness. In addition, giving the employee independent authority to write grievances creates difficulties for the management representatives, who must try to identify the real issues and respond directly to them. If a grievance is not clearly expressed, being properly responsive to it is difficult. The union's choices also significantly influence the functioning of the grievance procedure and suggest the degree to which training of its grievance representatives is required.

Too frequently union stewards have neither the authority nor the skills to settle grievances. Not untypically, lower-level supervisors have neither the authority nor the ability to settle grievances; the industrial relations department or, perhaps even worse, line managers retain all of the authority. In such instances, large grievance backlogs and less than constructive, if not antagonistic, relationships between the parties are frequent. Furthermore, representatives of both parties at the lower levels become dispirited and refuse to assume responsibility for the health of their relationship; their jobs are difficult enough to do anything other than kick grievances upstairs if that is where the authority to act resides. The bitter foreman who is required to reject all grievances and who then has his or her status with employees compromised when "higher-ups" grant the relief sought, frequently without prior warning or explanation, is an all too common personality.

Yet, even with the kind of training for which this book is designed, the prospects of resolving grievances, especially at the lower steps, should not be overestimated. Skilled stewards and supervisors can efficiently resolve relatively minor disputes that do not have significant contractual implications. But the supervisor, even if highly skilled in labor relations, is not an arbitrator and should not attempt, at the lower levels of authority, broad or technical interpretations of the agreement. Likewise the steward cannot make decisions about whether to drop or settle grievances at the early stages on the basis of his or her estimation of the chances of winning at arbitration. Such judgments need to be made by the parties, but at higher levels. Supervisors should deny grievances at the lowest levels when management rights are at issue or when policy interpretations of the agreement are necessary. Stewards should expect that cases involving important issues of contract interpretation pass beyond their level for resolution.

The objective of the parties need only be to provide the tools and support for representatives to resolve grievances at the lowest stage in the procedure appropriate for the issue. If settlements are beyond the scope of the representatives at any given level, at least they will understand their own roles, those of the individuals at higher levels, and the interdependence of all steps in the procedure. If that goal can be accomplished, the grievance procedure will work efficiently in the formal steps and the parties will be best equipped to resolve disputes as quickly as practicable and to protect their legitimate, vital interests.

MERIT REVIEW OF GRIEVANCES

Among the most sensitive problems that unions face in their role as exclusive bargaining agent is reviewing grievances on their merit. First, one of the most important and visible functions of the union is processing employee grievances. Second, when an individual employee has a grievance, he or she expects the union representatives to give it their full attention and support. Union members have little interest in having the bargaining agent to whom they pay dues inform them that a complaint, which is obviously valid to the employee, has little or no merit. As a result, the natural tendency for the union is to push grievances forward with each management rejection rather than to withdraw unmeritorious ones or settle weak ones with compromises. Although there are certainly budgetary and policy implications, it is relatively easy for management to give supervisors the authority to make compromise grievance settlements within their scope of responsibility. Safeguards, such as requiring consultation with industrial relations personnel and providing that any doubt should lead to rejection of the grievance, can be established. Still, since management can sustain the grievance at any level if it is so inclined, there is little harm in having lower-level supervisors reject it. Therefore, the natural tendency within both organizations tends to push grievances to the highest level, but deliberate pursuit of settlements at the lowest level probably poses more difficult problems for the union.

Somehow the union must deal with the political dilemma inherent in processing grievances. If it chooses to file and argue all grievances with equal vigor and without regard to merit, it will be impossible to negotiate compromise settlements on any of them. Management certainly will not consider all grievances equally important from its perspective and will have great difficulty evaluating which are more important to the union. Further, the primary management objective of promptly identifying and evaluating problems through the grievance procedure would be frustrated. Management cannot be expected to recognize the union's credibility if the union fails to take whatever steps are necessary to deal with grievances according to their relative merits. According to Elkouri: "No grievance should be presented unless there is a real basis for complaint or need for decision. Much responsibility belongs to the union stewards, and indirectly to the union, to screen out complaints that have no real merit."[9] Open confrontation is impossible if the union does not base its actions on merit review of grievances.[10] At the last step, as the Supreme Court has noted, arbitration "can function properly only if the grievance procedures leading to it can sift out unmeritorious claims."[11]

While the political problems are no less significant, the authority of a union to review grievances on their merits prior to demanding arbitration is even more clear than the authority to negotiate compromise settlements at lower steps in the procedure. The law provides that an individual employee can press a grievance through all internal steps in the grievance procedure without the intervention of the union. However, the effect of the *Trilogy* decisions has been that only the union has the right to arbitrate grievances. The union, not the individual employee, is party to the contract that creates arbitration, and the union bears the exclusive obligation of collective bargaining with the employer and for the costs of arbitration. Because arbitration is a risk, entails costs, and intimately affects the labor-management relationship, the union is under no obligation to take all grievances, even if meritorious, to arbitration. Its duty of fair representation does require, however, that the decision of whether to arbitrate a grievance must not be made in a manner that is arbitrary, discriminatory, or in bad faith.

While individual grievants may be able to understand why the union cannot arbitrate all grievances, they tend to find it more difficult to understand why the union should withdraw a grievance for lack of merit or agree to a compromise settlement at the lower steps. Yet political problems with individual dissatisfied members must be balanced against the great obstacle to union effectiveness that large grievance backlogs represent. In 1971 a joint committee of the United Steelworkers of America and five coordinating steel companies made a detailed examination of the processing of grievances in the steel industry, focusing on the problem of backlogs. The *Report of the Joint Study Committee* is especially significant because it recommended the expedited arbitration procedure that has worked so successfully for the steel industry and is discussed in more detail in Chapter 5. But the report is also significant for its forthright, joint recommendation that even if changes in local union bylaws are necessary, grievances without merit "must be taken out of the grievance procedure at the lowest possible step with a full explanation given to the grievant of why his grievance is not being filed or has been withdrawn."[12] However, the union's adoption of such an attitude has led to serious charges by more radical elements of the union that the leadership has "sold out" to management interests.[13]

Merit review of grievances is not a subject recognized only recently. In its 1943 publication *Preparing a Steward's Manual,* the U.S. Department of Labor recommended inclusion of the following instruction to stewards:

> *Use your best judgment in deciding whether or not a grievance is justified.*—If you are convinced that the worker does not have a real case, it is better to tell him so right from the beginning. Taking up a lot of poor cases will cost you the respect of all concerned. On the other hand, don't forget that you are the worker's representative. If the case is a borderline one but you feel that the worker has considerable justice on his side, tell him frankly that you are not sure what is the correct answer. Then take the case up and get a definite ruling through the grievance procedure.[14]

The ultimate yardstick for the union's decision must therefore be the merit of the grievance. To decide how to process a case on any other basis opens wide the door to an unfair representation charge. As the Supreme Court made clear in *Vaca* v. *Sipes,* merit review by the union during the lower stages of the grievance procedure is not only permissible but expected:

[I]n providing for a grievance and arbitration procedure which gives the union discretion to supervise the grievance machinery and to invoke arbitration, the employer and the union contemplate that each will endeavor in good faith to settle grievances short of arbitration. Through this settlement process, frivolous grievances are ended prior to the most costly and time-consuming step in the grievance procedure.[15]

However, evaluating the merits of a grievance for the purpose of deciding whether to file or forward it has nothing to do with the practical prospects for winning it. In meeting its fair representation duty, a union must pursue a grievance with merit even if it is absolutely convinced that management will deny the relief sought and that the case is not strong enough contractually for the union to arbitrate. The union should be convinced that the grievance is frivolous or otherwise totally lacking in merit before refusing to file or process it. Any doubts should be resolved in favor of proceeding with the grievance, at least at the early steps, and treating it thereafter in a manner that is not arbitrary, discriminatory, in bad faith, or negligent. In order to provide an additional measure of legal protection, unions may wish to develop an internal appeal procedure so that a single steward or officer cannot arbitrarily dispose of a grievance on his or her own authority. Local union bylaws might provide that the decision not to file a grievance or not to proceed with it can be appealed to a grievance committee for review. If the decision to proceed or not is already made by a grievance committee, bylaws might provide that the committee's decision could be appealed to the executive committee. Such an appeal procedure should be sufficient to protect a union from unfair representation charges arising from a refusal to proceed with a grievance.

Because the union supervises the grievance procedure and is the acting party in moving disputes forward, this chapter has necessarily focused on union concerns. If the procedure is to work effectively, union representatives must understand these issues and management representatives must recognize the union's objectives and functions in evaluating their own course of action. Chapter 4 deals more specifically with issues related to union's presentation of grievances and management's response to grievances.

Reference Notes

[1] *United Steelworkers of America* v. *Warrior & Gulf Navigation Co.*, 363 U.S. 574 (1960).
[2] Beeler, *Roles of the Labor Leader*, 22.
[3] *Ibid.*, 24-25.
[4] *Vaca* v. *Sipes*, 383 U.S. 171 (1967).
[5] Beeler, *Roles of the Labor Leader*, 22-23.
[6] *Ibid.*, 27.
[7] 49 Stat. 449 (1935).
[8] Beeler, *Roles of the Labor Leader*, 20.

[9]Elkouri, *How Arbitration Works,* 110.

[10]*Ibid.,* 111.

[11]*NLRB* v. *Acme Industrial Co.,* 385 U.S. 432 (1967).

[12]Coordinating Steel Companies and United Steelworkers of America, "Report of the Joint Study Committee on Grievance and Arbitration Procedure, (June 14, 1971), 17.

[13]See, for example, Charles Spencer, *Blue Collar* (Chicago: Lakeside Charter Books, 1977).

[14]Quoted in Elkouri, *How Arbitration Works,* 110-111.

[15]*Vaca* v. *Sipes,* 383 U.S. 171 (1967).

CHAPTER 4

Processing Grievances

Since evidence, facts, and coherent arguments are essential to the grievance resolution process, the representatives of both parties must be skilled investigators. In addition, union representatives must be proficient in writing and presenting grievances, and management representatives, competent in conducting grievance meetings and writing grievance responses. All individuals involved in the grievance procedure need highly developed listening skills in order to cut through hesitancy, deceptiveness, and bravado to "hear" the real problem. Active listening requires understanding feelings as well as hearing spoken words—the ability to read between the lines. The ability to listen actively also contributes to the final essential quality of an effective grievance representative: empathy, the ability to understand intimately the thoughts, feelings, and motives of another party from that person's point of view. Individuals who can demonstrate empathy are people who appear to be open, fair, genuine, confident, and competent. Further, being able to see an issue from the point of view of the other party contributes enormously to the development of a strategy to counter the other party. In the adversary arena of the grievance-arbitration procedure, the best way to formulate a defense against the other party's case is to anticipate the other party's likely offense.

INVESTIGATING GRIEVANCES

A grievance cannot be understood and evaluated, much less resolved, without an investigation of the facts surrounding it. Investigation includes systematic observation or examination of the facts of a case as well as research into the labor relations principles that govern the issues raised.

Ironically, despite its fundamental importance, investigation is the task that both union and management representatives probably do least well. All too often, a grievance isn't thoroughly investigated until arbitration, and sometimes not even then. Both union and management will be best prepared for their roles in the grievance procedure as well as for their roles at arbitration if they treat each grievance from the first formal step as one that may be arbitrated. The grievance procedure itself then produces a full development of the facts and arguments in a case so that by the last internal step, the parties are in the best possible position to assess the benefits and risks of settling. Even if the parties typically retain counsel to present cases at arbitration, the case can be much more effectively (and cheaply) prepared by the legal representatives if it has been fully developed in the grievance procedure.

Although the steward investigates a grievance first, sometimes before the management supervisor is even aware that a complaint may arise, both must ultimately secure the same basic information:

- Who was involved?
- What happened which led to the grievance?
- When did the incident or action occur?
- Where did relevant events take place?
- Why did all relevant actions occur?
- How were relevant actions taken?

For the steward, the most crucial part of investigating an individual grievance frequently is interviewing the grievant. Often the steward must deal with an emotional, even irrational, employee; the initial complaint may be only a symptom of the real problem. Union stewards can be credible and effective as advocates for their members only to the extent that they can demonstrate an empathetic understanding of the employee's feelings and an appreciation for the stake the employee has in the dispute. While the steward should certainly promise the employee a complete investigation, promising the full support of the union for the employee's case at this early stage in the investigation is overzealous and politically dangerous. The union may indeed be in the position of later informing the member that the grievance has little merit, no matter how justified the complaint may be from a standard of fairness, and that "winning" is unlikely.

Besides interviewing the grievant, a steward may also have to locate and interview any witnesses. Since two people rarely see or hear the same event in exactly the same way, the steward may have to weigh conflicting evidence in order to construct the most reliable account. Employer disciplinary, attendance, or other records may have to be checked. If prior offenses or warnings are likely to be part of management's justification for disciplinary action, the exact nature and dates of those events may be important. A union that fails to investigate evidence concerning grievances in a diligent manner may breach the duty of fair representation by its negligence.[1] Because grievance processing is included within the legal duty to bargain, all information reasonably necessary to the union's fulfillment of its responsibilities must be accessible. The National Labor Relations Board has ruled consistently that employers must supply promptly and in reasonably useful form all such relevant and necessary information upon a good faith demand from the union.[2]

In addition to interviewing the grievant and witnesses and examining records, the steward must consult with other union officials. A steward may have to discuss an issue of contract interpretation with a union officer, business agent, or international staff representative. Members of the negotiating team may have to be consulted to determine the union's outlook on an issue or the intent of the parties. It may be useful to talk with other stewards to determine whether similar situations have arisen, possibly at other work sites. Uncovering inconsistent management behavior may win a case.

Beyond gathering facts, investigation also requires two kinds of research. First, the union representative should determine whether any grievances have arisen on the same subject before. If so, what did the union argue; how did management respond; what was the outcome? If similar cases went to arbitration, the arbitrator's award will be important. Indeed, if there has been a prior award on the same point and the contract language is unchanged, that award should dispose of the grievance. Second, the union representative should research the arbitration principles applicable to the issue being grieved. More infrequently than not, union as well as management representatives overlook this step. For example, if the grievance charges that management did not discipline for just cause, it is important to know the meaning of the just cause standard so that facts, evidence, and arguments can be developed in light of the tests that an arbitrator will most likely use. Such research can be accomplished using the arbitration-case-reporting services and other published materials on the grievance-arbitration procedure issued by the Bureau of National Affairs, Labor Arbitration Information Service, Commerce Clearing House, and Prentice-Hall. Books such as *How Arbitration Works* by Elkouri and Elkouri and *Evidence in Arbitration* by Hill and Sinicropi are also useful.[3]

The union ought to organize its case around the arbitration standards appropriate for any particular grievance because that process greatly aids the full development of the argument. The union will be in the position to present the strongest possible case to management; by forcing management to weigh its own case against the usual arbitration standards, the union may be able to encourage movement toward a settlement. Moreover, if the grievance is not resolved, the union will have a valuable aid in the decision of whether to arbitrate. If the decision is affirmative, much of the arbitration case will already have been developed.

Upon receipt of the grievance, management's representative should undertake the same kind of research as the union representatives. Management will probably not interview the grievant but will want to interview the supervisor and any other nonbargaining unit personnel involved. In some circumstances, management may also interview bargaining unit members, but the standard expectation is that bargaining unit members will not testify against each other. For the same reasons that apply to the union, the management representative should consult others in the line of command as well as the industrial relations department in order to learn about appropriate policy interpretations, negotiation history, prior grievances, and arbitration awards. Similarly, management representatives should—but all too often don't—research the applicable standards at arbitration. Clearly, management is in the best position to judge whether to offer a grievance settlement or to reject the grievance if it can assess, as accurately as possible, its prospects with arbitration.

After gathering all relevant facts, interviewing witnesses, and researching the grievance issue, each party should conclude the investigation phase by preparing the best possible case for the other side. Only in this way can the representatives be certain that they are in a position to make the strongest possible arguments for their respective positions and against the positions of the other side.

The task of investigation extends throughout the grievance procedure. Obviously, if the other party uses unanticipated evidence or arguments, further investigation must be done. Beyond the need to seek additional information when necessary, this investigation process is rarely completed prior to the final internal steps of the grievance procedure. Indeed, the early steps, particularly the informal stage and the first formal step, are important parts of the investigation itself since each party hears the viewpoint of the other for the first time. By the time the parties meet at the lowest level where the grievance could actually be resolved and certainly at the last internal step prior to arbitration, the investigation should be complete. By then, each party should have developed a theory of the case— the single, most comprehensive and persuasive account of the circumstances that can be supported by facts and evidence and supports its contentions in the grievance. Nothing should be held back in the argument. With arbitration the only remaining alternative if the grievance is not resolved, each party must be prepared to present the strongest possible case.

WRITING GRIEVANCES: UNION

Usually the parties agree upon a form to be used for written grievances; while formats vary widely in practice, content is relatively consistent. A model grievance form completed for a hypothetical grievance is shown in Figure 4-2. Written grievance forms usually begin with necessary background information such as name of the grievant, department, classification or job title, clock number, and work site. If more than one individual is grieving the same issue, all should be specified unless the union itself is filing a group or policy grievance on their behalf.

FIGURE 4-2
Standard Grievance Record Form, Step 1

GRIEVANCE NUMBER *82-003*   DATE FILED *4/23/82*   UNION *Local 1233*

NAME OF GRIEVANT(S) *Flacko, George*   CLOCK # *0379*

DATE CAUSE OF GRIEVANCE OCCURRED   *4/20/82*

CONTRACTUAL PROVISIONS CITED   *Articles III, VII, and others*

STATEMENT OF THE GRIEVANCE:

    On April 20, Foreman Pat Zajac asked George Flacko to go temporarily to the Rolling Mill for the rest of the turn. Flacko said he preferred not to, and that he was more senior to others who were available. The foreman never ordered Flacko to take the temporary assignment. He only requested that Flacko do so.

    Flacko was improperly charged with insubordination and suspended for three days. The foreman did not have just cause for the discipline.

RELIEF SOUGHT:

    Reinstatement with full back pay and seniority.

GRIEVANT'S SIGNATURE ___*George Flacko*___ DATE *4/22/82*

STEWARD'S SIGNATURE ___*Paul Smith*___ DATE *4/23/82*

STEP 1

DISPOSITION:

    Foreman Zajac gave Flacko clear instructions to report temporarily to the Rolling Mill for the remainder of the shift. Flacko refused to do so and was warned that it could result in discipline. When he again refused the foreman's directive, he was disciplined.

    The discipline was for just cause. The grievance is rejected.

SIGNATURE OF EMPLOYER REPRESENTATIVE ___*J. K. Ellis*___ DATE *4/26/82*

_____ Grievance Withdrawn   or   ✓ Referred to Step 2

SIGNATURE OF UNION REPRESENTATIVE ___*Paul Smith*___ DATE *4/28/82*

The first information required with a possible bearing on the outcome of the grievance is the date of its cause. Since agreements frequently establish a time limit for filing grievances, the date is important as evidence of the timeliness of the grievance. If a particular incident or management action resulted in the grievance, establishing the date will be relatively simple. If the agreement stipulates that the time limit begins when the grievant knew or "should have known" about the circumstances initiating the complaint, there may be considerable room for disagreement. Further, some grievances, such as those alleging discrimination, may be focused more on an apparent continuing violation rather than upon some individual action.

Almost all grievance forms require an indication of the allegedly violated provisions of the collective bargaining agreement. The parties usually agree that at the point a grievance must be reduced to writing, the issue should be specified so that the dispute can be narrowed. Specifying all applicable articles is important for the union because unless the agreement provides otherwise, modifications may not be permitted in later steps. Since much investigation is likely after the filing of the formal grievance, which conceivably could open new areas of argument, the union should take care to stipulate all possible provisions under which it may have grounds to raise objection. Indeed, in order to provide some flexibility, it is common for the steward to add *and others* after the provisions specifically cited. Moreover, in some circumstances the union may wish to base the grievance on the entire contract or the spirit of the agreement rather than some specific section. If the dispute involves the overall relationship between the parties, this may be the only way to write the grievance. On the other hand, such a tactic could reflect an inability to find specific grounds in the contract for the complaint.

The union's flexibility in specifying contract violations depends upon the contractual definition of a grievance and the practice of the parties in processing grievances. If the agreement does not explicitly permit the union to modify the grievance at later stages and the union is permitted to add alleged violations as the grievance is being processed, it will be difficult for management suddenly to insist that all violations be alleged at the time of filing. While the union representative probably should try to keep the area of potential argument in support of the grievance as wide as possible, the management representative should try to narrow the issue to the specific grounds for dispute as quickly as possible.

After indicating contractual violations by section, the union representative must then describe the nature of the grievance as concisely as possible. Arguments and evidence are not appropriate; they will be made in meetings when the grievance is discussed. Supplying arguments would not only tip the union's hand too early but also limit the union in the lines of argument that it might ultimately wish to use. Furthermore, by writing too much, the union representative may make some factual or interpretive error that will have a damaging impact in later grievance meetings. What should be provided is a concise summary of the events or actions giving rise to the grievance and a brief statement of how the contract was allegedly violated.

The last item that must be supplied is a statement of the relief being sought. Only that relief necessary to correct the alleged wrong—to make the grievant "whole"—is appropriate. The relief should go no further than to reestablish equity under the agreement or to reestablish the conditions that would have been in place had the violation not occurred. Thus, a grievance alleging discipline without just cause would seek not only a retraction of the discipline but also payment of all monies lost and restoration of any seniority lost. If the grievance alleges that a grievant was improperly compensated for a job assignment, payment at the proper rate for all hours worked is appropriate but interest or punitive damages are not. As another illustration, a union cannot appropriately seek an apology from a supervisor for improper discipline or request management to discipline the supervisor, even though some grievants want that result. Such decisions are properly within management's sphere of action.

The union should take special care to indicate all persons or all job classifications entitled to relief should the grievance be allowed. Too frequently, the union fails to indicate the proper scope of the grievance. It is not at all uncommon in the arbitration of a grievance charging that a foreman did bargaining unit work to discover that the union has not specified who is entitled to compensation. Since the arbitrator may not dispense his or her own brand of industrial justice and is limited to a consideration of the issue presented and the language of the contract, a union should not expect the arbitrator to determine which persons are eligible for relief. Carelessness on this point may have the result that even though a number of employees were harmed, only the employee actually filing the grievance receives relief. Such a result can obviously harm the union in the eyes of its members. Furthermore, a failure to specify the complete scope of relief may communicate weakness in a case to an arbitrator.

Once the form is completed and any necessary signatures are secured, the union representative files the grievance in whatever manner the parties determine. Management's investigation then begins, and both parties prepare for discussion of the issue at the first grievance meeting.

PRESENTING GRIEVANCES: UNION

Within any time limits specified in the contract but after the management representative has conducted at least an initial investigation, the parties schedule a grievance meeting. Usually both parties are still actively investigating the issues in dispute even while the early grievance meetings are being scheduled. As a result, neither the union's presentation nor management's response will be as fully developed as they will be by the last formal step. Almost invariably, grievances involving contract interpretation rise to higher steps in the procedure since they involve policy questions. But in the case of less complex grievances, the union should be able to present at the lower levels its view of what happened, how the contract was violated, and what actions are required to resolve the dispute. The following suggestions apply to grievance meetings at all steps. In reality, they usually characterize only presentations at the later steps, if at all.

To begin with, the steward must prepare the case before the meeting. This preparation requires not only developing the union's arguments but also anticipating management's responses so that they can be counteracted. If the grievant is to be present at the meeting, the steward should discuss the entire presentation with him or her in advance, indicating what information the grievant may be asked to supply, if any, and reviewing the grievant's responses to questions that will be asked. The steward should also prepare the grievant for questions that management may ask; together they should determine whether the steward will make all statements and responses or if the grievant is free to respond to questions.

Whether the grievant is present is usually a procedural issue for the union. Even if the grievant normally attends, in some cases it might be wise for the grievant to be absent. In establishing its procedure, however, the union should carefully consider the therapeutic value of the grievance procedure and the value of having the employee participate in his or her "day in court." Having grievants witness effectively argued cases in grievance meetings is often of great value regardless of the outcome.

The steward should probably present the case as spokesperson for the union and the grievant. Just as the man who acts as his own lawyer has a fool for a client, letting the grievant present the case personally probably reduces the effectiveness of the case. Not only does the grievant have a clearly vested interest in the outcome, he or she is likely to be involved at least somewhat emotionally—a factor that could be exploited by management's representatives at some point in the meeting. Most employees are not skilled in labor relations matters, particularly standards for contract interpretation. A grievant may not say enough to support a major point or may say too much. For all these reasons, it is probably best for the union to present the case. At all costs, those participating for the union should avoid expressions of difference or disagreement at the meeting. Should differences develop, a recess should be requested in order to agree upon a united front.

Persuasiveness characterizes the effective grievance presentation. The union advocate must stick to the point of the grievance and not be drawn into arguments with management or into discussions of irrelevant issues. The issue and the union's or grievant's contentions should be stated clearly; the steward should try constantly to narrow the differences between the union and management positions. Throughout the meeting, the union's position on the grievance should be maintained; there is always time later to withdraw the grievance if facts that fatally undermine the case are presented. Seeking a quick and complete resolution at the lowest possible step in the grievance procedure should be the context for the union's presentation.

Depending upon the relationship between the parties in general and their representatives at any given step, possible areas of settlement may be explored either explicitly or obliquely at the meeting. Rarely do either union or management offer a compromise initially, since doing so would tend to undermine their negotiating position should the compromise be unsatisfactory. Thus, the union might indicate subtly the sort of settlement short of the full relief sought that might be acceptable, or management might "hypothetically" present a response implying a compromise in order to get the union's reaction. Most often, compromise settlements grow from later, less official contacts between the parties rather than from actual negotiations in grievance meetings. Usually both representatives must consult others within their organizations before determining whether a settlement can be offered or accepted.

When the issues have been thoroughly discussed, the meeting ends and management's representative must begin to prepare a written response within the contractually specified time limits.

CONDUCTING GRIEVANCE MEETINGS: MANAGEMENT

While the parties come to a grievance meeting as equals, the meeting itself is frequently conducted by the management representative. Often the meeting opens with the supervisor reviewing the grievance and the factual circumstances and then asking the union to explain the grievance. While he or she is clearly an advocate, the management representative has the responsibility to conduct the meeting fairly and to ensure that all relevant facts are made known.

Therefore, how the management representative conducts grievance meetings can have a considerable influence on the atmosphere of labor-management relations in general and the tone of the grievance meeting in particular. A supervisor who is obviously hostile, who demonstrates resentment at having to take the time to conduct the meeting, or who is interruptive and argumentative, will not be considered fair. It should be important to both parties that the union and grievant leave the meeting with the conviction that the manager listened with sincere interest, understood the union's contentions and the evidence and arguments for them, avoided snap judgments, and respected the rights of the grievant and the authority of the union.

Highly developed human relations and communications skills are essential for the advocates of both parties but especially significant for the manager who conducts grievance meetings. Active listening and empathy are imperative. The management representative must be able to cut through the emotionalism of an angry employee and the rhetoric of an overly aggressive or threatening union presentation to get to the real dispute in order to understand the grievance and evaluate its merits. The complaint may not be important at all, or it may be a symptom of another problem or a larger one. Without question, if complaints and grievances are not distinguished at the informal step, they must be by the first formal step. As Harry W. Lacey, a management spokesperson, describes the task of management's representative:

> Greater emphasis should be placed on training foremen in the human relations aspects of their jobs. Many times a man simply wants a relief hour or perhaps a sympathetic listener. Foremen must be given better training on the importance of fully hearing out rather than prematurely debating with their employees. They must acquire the ability of [noting] *what* is being said, rather than the manner in which the problem is being presented. Only in this way can gripes be separated from grievances, or can gripes be kept from becoming grievances.[4]

The management representative should avoid starting or being drawn into arguments about the grievance issue and must recognize the therapeutic function of the meeting in allowing the grievant to let off steam, either personally or by participating in the union's presentation of the case.

Management's representative cannot escape the dilemma of being both an advocate for management's legitimate interests and an objective participant. At the earliest opportunity, he or she should seek to narrow the grievance to its basic issues. If the union has broadly specified the grounds for the grievance, such as by indicating violations of Articles III, VII, and others, the manager should force the union to identify specifically the relevant provisions. Questions must be asked deliberately, clearly, and nonjudgmentally in order to elicit clear responses from the union. Besides identifying the problem, the manager's role is to evaluate the strength of the grievance in contractual terms and to try to gauge the degree of union support for it. An inability to state the problem clearly might indicate that the union is only going through the motions of presenting a case that it knows is weak or that the union is bluffing. If the union is arguing with unusual vigor in a case that seems obviously weak, management's representative should try to discern the reason. Is it, for example, essentially a political grievance?

When the management representative is satisfied that no more can be learned about the grievance and the union representative is satisfied that he or she has made a full presentation, the grievance meeting ends. Only a careful investigation of the issue and response according to the time limits of the grievance procedure should be promised.

RESPONDING TO GRIEVANCES: MANAGEMENT

Overemphasizing the importance of consultation with line managers and the industrial relations department before preparing a written grievance response is impossible. Only consultation allows higher management to coordinate labor relations policies, protect against the establishment of unfavorable practices, confront employee problems, and monitor management's response. For the management representative at any stage in the grievance procedure, but especially at the lower steps, consultation is the mechanism for discovering management's view of the contract language in question; relevant previous grievances and arbitration awards; pertinent rules, procedures, practices, and laws; and applicable arbitration principles. Besides consultation, the management representative must conduct any necessary further research, review timeliness standards, weigh the argument and evidence presented on behalf of the grievant, and frame a response. Depending upon management policy, the response may have to be reviewed by higher authority before it is issued.

Management's response, like the union's statement of the grievance, will become an official statement of its basic position for the record. While neither the grievance nor the response should contain the arguments of the parties, what is written can materially affect the outcome of the grievance. The response should therefore be accurate and concise. Possibly higher management has ordered a rejection so that the grievance can be advanced to higher, more appropriate levels. If so, the rejection should be firm, direct, and very brief. If the problem is an easy one to settle or if the grievant is obviously correct, the response should allow the grievance and order relief as concisely as possible without apology or rationalization. In the event of a negotiated settlement, the response should embody the compromise agreement, but in no case should the response offer or describe a compromise that the union has not already accepted, at least implicitly. For example, if it is not certain that a reduction in discipline, rather than its complete retraction, will result in resolution of the grievance, the reduction should not be offered in the grievance response. If the offer has been made but not accepted, the grievance should be rejected without reference to the compromise discussions.

There is disagreement about how completely a grievance response should state management's position. But there is general agreement that a response should neither be argumentative nor so long that the manager writes too much, thereby damaging the case at higher levels. In general, management should be directly responsive to the union's grievance. For instance, if the union simply stated that "disciplinary action was without just cause," the manager might appropriately respond, "Grievance denied. Management had just cause for discipline." However, if the grievance provided details of management's alleged failure to discipline for just cause, the main points of the grievance should be addressed in the response. If management disagrees with the union's version of the facts of the case, the factual dispute should be noted in the response. Without being argumentative but still responding directly to the grievance, the reply should communicate management's rationale as concisely as possible.

As the grievance moves through the steps of the grievance procedure, management will be naturally inclined to support its personnel and their actions or decisions. Not to assume such support would create or reflect serious morale problems within the management structure. Nevertheless, if it does become clear at higher steps in the procedure that a supervisor or other representative of management acted incorrectly, management will probably want to seek some nonprecedential, compromise settlement or even to allow the grievance on a nonprecedential basis, as indicated clearly in the written response. The matter of poor judgment must then be handled directly with the management personnel involved in the most effective and appropriate manner for each individual. Obviously, management must always be able to assure its supervisors that it will not deliberately undercut them in full view of the employees whom they supervise and the union. Hopefully, errors will be explained and the actions expected in similar future situations will be addressed. While usually overlooked, there is also enormous reinforcement value in explicit recognition by higher management of correct contract administration actions by supervisors.

CONSIDERING ARBITRATION

Prior to writing its final grievance response, if not before, management must evaluate the prospect of the union's demanding arbitration and of the likely outcome. If fundamental management rights are involved, management must stand firm despite the risks of arbitration. However, if important but less than fundamental interests are at stake, management must weigh the full range of factors before deciding simply to reject the grievance or actively to pursue a compromise settlement. Likewise, the union must evaluate its chances at arbitration in deciding whether to pursue actively some compromise settlement or accept one, if offered. If management rejects the grievance outright, the union also must weigh the full range of factors before deciding whether to demand arbitration.

Hopefully, both parties will have developed their cases fully by the last step in the grievance procedure so that their actions are taken in light of what they believe to be the prospects of arbitration. While this is not often the case in reality, there is universal agreement that it should be. In order for arbitration to work efficiently in providing final resolution to grievances, it should be reserved by the parties primarily for those disputes that raise complex or difficult problems of interpretation on which they have been unable to agree despite their best efforts. Certainly disputes will continue to be advanced to arbitration for political reasons. A union, if it can possibly afford to do so, will probably arbitrate all discharge and discrimination cases in order to minimize the risk of fair representation problems in those sensitive areas. Management will frequently decide that it must take its chances at arbitration because a particular supervisor must be backed or because the highest levels of authority have rejected possible compromises. These exceptions aside, there is clear agreement that the parties should endeavor to arbitrate only those cases that reflect important, irreconcilable disputes.

Although they will view the decision at the last internal step of the grievance procedure from differing perspectives, both parties should consider the same issues in deciding whether to demand arbitration (union) or risk arbitration by denying the grievance (management).

1. Are we convinced that our interpretation of the agreement is correct?
2. Is the issue important enough to risk arbitration?
3. What would be the effect of winning?
4. What would be the effect of losing?
5. Can we afford the cost and the delay in final resolution?
6. Based on known arbitration principles and what we know about the case of the other party and our own, can we win?

Reference Notes

[1] See *Hines* v. *Anchor Motor Freight*, 424 U.S. 554 (1976).
[2] For a thorough discussion of relevant cases, see Charles J. Morris ed., *The Developing Labor Law* (Washington, D.C.: Bureau of National Affairs, 1971), 309-316.
[3] Elkouri, *How Arbitration Works;* Marvin Hill and Anthony Sinicropi, *Evidence in Arbitration* (Washington, D.C.: Bureau of National Affairs, 1980). See also Hill and Sinicropi, *Remedies in Arbitration* (Washington, D.C.: Bureau of National Affairs, 1981).
[4] Harry W. Lacey, *Proceedings of the Conference on Improving Relations between the Parties*, 29 (University of Notre Dame Press, 1960), as quoted in Elkouri, *How Arbitration Works,* 111.

CHAPTER 5

Grievance Arbitration

Students of labor relations sometimes get the erroneous impression that arbitration is a method of resolving conflicts used exclusively to settle disputes between management and labor. Nothing could be further from the truth. Arbitration is used extensively outside the labor-management arena to resolve an ever increasing variety of commercial and civil matters. In the commercial world, arbitration is often utilized as a private system of dispute resolution that provides an alternative to formal litigation.

The following example illustrates the use of arbitration as an alternative to litigation. Suppose that a merchant and his supplier are involved in an irreconcilable dispute involving the quality of goods supplied. This dispute could be resolved by civil litigation if either party initiated a lawsuit. Use of the courts, however, exacts a high price from both litigants in the form of time and expense. If the suit is of any consequence, the parties will be compelled to file formal pleadings and adhere to strict time limits. There may be an extensive discovery process that entails depositions and written interrogatories. Representation by counsel is a virtual necessity; vast sums may be expended on preparation long before the case approaches trial. The rules of procedure are strict and permit few shortcuts. Aside from these formalities, the parties will encounter long delays due to crowded court calendars; in some areas the case may not reach trial for three or four years.

As an alternative to the courts, suppose that the merchant and the supplier decided to submit the dispute to a neutral third party and to be bound by the decision. They could select their "judge," prescribe limits to the arbitrator's authority, and to a large degree dictate the procedure under which the dispute would be tried. They could stipulate the issue, agree to dispense with transcripts and briefs, and ask for an advance commitment from the arbitrator to submit a short explanatory decision within 30 days of the hearing. The advantage of arbitration becomes all too obvious: the parties are no longer at the mercy of the courts and the formal rules of civil procedure. They are instead in a position, if they use discretion, to exercise a great deal of control over the proceeding.

There are also definite and distinct disadvantages of arbitration. These are all too often overlooked because, unlike the advantages, they are not obvious. First and foremost is the fact that any given arbitrator's future with the parties depends on his or her ability to please both of the litigants. If either party is convinced that the arbitrator did not act fairly, that arbitrator is finished insofar as that party is concerned. Assuming that the losing party is reasonably sophisticated, there is always the possibility that the arbitrator can explain and justify his or her conclusions in a well-reasoned opinion. Moreover, a truly sophisticated party generally will prefer an arbitrator who will courageously follow his or her convictions over one who is known to split decisions. However, a primary objective of an arbitrator must be to convince both the winner and the loser that he or she was fair; by any standards, that is certainly a difficult task. Despite the denials of the arbitration fraternity, there always will be some suspicion that there is a tendency to split and compromise decisions in a system where the arbitrator must be mutually selected and costs are shared equally by both sides. Judges, on the other hand, have little concern with maintaining a flow of cases; that is the least of their problems. Moreover, after completing a case, the chances are excellent that the judge will never have any contact with the litigants. Thus, the objective of a judge is not to please both sides or either side; instead, he or she is concerned primarily with correctly applying the law. This is not to say that arbitrators are less honest than judges. To the contrary, most arbitrators try to decide each case fairly by correctly applying the contract. Yet it would be naive to believe that there may not be some suspicion that the arbitration profession tries too hard to accommodate both parties and that this tempers justice.

A second advantage or disadvantage of arbitration, depending on one's point of view, is that, except for gross error or corruption, there is little chance to appeal an adverse arbitration decision. Thus, the parties occasionally are stuck with an incredible decision. At times, the lack of finality due to the appeal procedure in the court system is a source of frustration and is seen as a distinct disadvantage of formal litigation. However, the appeal procedure, and for that matter most rules of civil procedure, have been included in the court structure for a single, laudable purpose: to ensure that both parties receive a fair and impartial trial. A price occasionally must be paid when these safeguards are sacrificed for the informality and expedience of arbitration.

A third disadvantage of arbitration, also related to the lack of an appeal system, is the fact that arbitration is far less consistent and predictable than formal litigation. Since arbitrators are not bound to follow established precedent, there is simply no way to be certain how an arbitrator will handle a given issue. The problem is compounded by the lack of formal licensing or educational requirement to become an arbitrator; anyone who is mutually selected can serve. As a result, there is an embarrassing lack of agreement among arbitrators with regard to many basic and critical questions. This is another price that must be paid when resorting to a private system of dispute resolution.

This frustrating lack of consistency among arbitrators becomes all too apparent when one reads a text on arbitration, such as the respected *How Arbitration Works* by Elkouri and Elkouri. Chapter after chapter is replete with notations on areas of disagreement regarding basic principles among arbitrators. For example, in a dispute over whether a senior employee meets the qualification requirements of a certain contract, there is some difference of opinion as to which party has the burden of proof.[1] Is the burden on the employer to prove that the bypassed employee *was not* qualified, or must the grievant prove that he or she *was* qualified? Such questions become settled with finality when a high court deals with the issue. Once settled, lower courts are bound to honor the precedent. Arbitrators, on the other hand, remain free to ignore precedent, resulting in many different opinions within the arbitration community. This lack of consistency makes arbitration an unsuitable forum for certain purposes. (The problem of using arbitration to enforce the law has been mentioned in Chapter 2.) Using arbitration as a forum to give meaning to ambiguous legal terms such as *sexual harassment* has definite limitations. Without a doubt, there would be a variety of different opinions as to the essential elements of such an offense.

ARBITRATION AND THE COURTS

In the preceding example of the commercial dispute between a merchant and the supplier, the arbitration process was an alternative to formal litigation. There is certainly nothing wrong with using arbitration for that purpose; virtually every state has passed legislation that permits or condones the use of arbitration by private parties. While the use of arbitration to resolve certain types of disputes is considered proper, indeed desirable, in certain situations, it was long regarded as an extraordinary system of jurisprudence. The idea of being bound, without appeal, to the decision of a third party whose only qualification was mutual selection was not taken lightly. Because of the somewhat extraordinary nature of the process, the courts tended to give arbitration clauses a narrow construction. This narrow interpretation holds that a party should not be *compelled* to submit to arbitration in the absence of a clear agreement to do so beforehand and any doubt in this regard should be resolved against arbitration.

Assume that the merchant and the supplier had entered an agreement to submit to arbitration all unresolved disputes relating to quality of goods supplied. Further assume that such a dispute arose but the supplier refused to honor the agreement to arbitrate. The remedy for the merchant would be to take the supplier into court and to ask the court to order the supplier to do what he agreed to do: arbitrate. The court would carefully examine the arbitration clause and determine the nature of the dispute to make certain that it fell within the scope of the agreement to arbitrate. In such a situation, the court would order arbitration only if there were a clear and positive commitment on the part of both parties to arbitrate and all doubt would be resolved against arbitration.

GRIEVANCE ARBITRATION
UNDER A LABOR AGREEMENT

In the negotiation of a labor agreement, it is virtually impossible to anticipate every contingency and avoid all ambiguity so as to preclude absolutely questions or disputes that might arise. If a labor contract is conceived as a code that governs the total relationship between the employer and the employees, the futility of trying to anticipate every problem or circumstance while the agreement is in effect should be obvious.[2] For example, the contract may provide that if death occurs in the employee's immediate family, the employee is entitled to paid leave while attending the funeral. Even seemingly clear language such as this is apt to spawn disputes. Social customs are changing; it is not unusual for men and women to live together as if they were married without legal formalities. Is such a companion a member of the immediate family?

If a death occurs while the employee is on vacation, the company may take the position that the vacationing employee is not entitled to funeral leave because he or she is able to attend the funeral without loss of pay. The union, on the other hand, may respond that funeral leave is a negotiated benefit; if a covered death occurs during vacation, the employee is entitled to both vacation *and* paid funeral leave. As the parties become more sophisticated at negotiation, their ability to anticipate and foresee problems of this nature increases, and they become more adept at drafting language that covers such contingencies. But no matter how experienced the negotiators may be, some unforeseen events are likely during the administration of the agreement.

Aside from the unforeseen, the parties frequently and deliberately will include language in a contract, knowing full well that it is ambiguous. An excellent example would be the typical just-cause provision that usually limits management's right to discipline employees. Both the company and the union will agree that management may impose discipline if there is just cause. However, there would be considerable disagreement if they attempted to specify exactly what constituted just cause. Realizing that such an endeavor could bog down negotiations, both parties may desire to facilitate agreement by simply stating that the company may discipline for just cause. Similarly many contracts simply state that seniority will be the determining factor, provided that the senior bidder is qualified. Obviously, terms such as *just cause* and *qualified* are, at best, ambiguous and therefore open invitation to controversy when applied to specific situations. Yet virtually all negotiators would agree that the desirability of obtaining an agreement in a reasonable time, thus avoiding a strike, far outweighs any advantage possible from the almost impossible task of eliminating all ambiguity from the agreement. Indeed, in order to give the parties some flexibility with regard to specific situations, some ambiguity actually may be desirable.

Since some differences of opinion are expected regarding the interpretation or application of an agreement during its term, some method must exist for the resolution of conflict. In a mature labor-management relationship one would hope that most differences of opinion are resolved by the parties themselves in the grievance procedure. In this regard the duty to bargain does not terminate with the signing of the contract but continues with the application and interpretation of the agreement. In this sense the processing and discussion of grievances are a continuation of collective bargaining, which is protected by law.[3] The best barometer to measure the sophistication of the parties is not how many grievances are filed but is instead the parties' ability to find workable resolutions to their conflicts. Many industrial relations managers place less emphasis on winning a particular grievance than on obtaining a mutually agreeable solution for the resolution of future problems. They are more than willing to compromise on a particular legitimate claim, provided that certain guidelines will apply in the future.

Unfortunately, no matter how adept the parties may be at finding mutually acceptable solutions to problems that arise during the term of the agreement, some disputes simply cannot be reconciled. Aside from legitimate differences of opinion regarding interpretation or application, sometimes internal political considerations may force either or both of the parties into a position from which there is no retreat. For example, it might not be politically expedient for a union to withdraw support from a discharged member. The company may be locked into its position by the belief that it must back one of its supervisors.

The potential for some disputes during the term of the agreement that cannot be resolved by the parties themselves obviously requires some procedure for final resolution. Years ago, unions relied on a rather straightforward method to enforce the contract. If, in the opinion of the union, the company failed to live up to its contractual obligations, the union called a strike. This assumed (as was usually the case) that the union had not waived its right to strike during the term of the contract by including a no-strike clause in the agreement.

Relying on the strike weapon to enforce agreements imposes several disadvantages on both parties. First, from the company's point of view, the one reward that it hopes to obtain from concessions at the bargaining table is a period of labor peace during the term of the agreement. The prospect of production being interrupted by spasmodic strikes over unresolved grievances generally makes the use of strikes as a dispute settlement method totally unacceptable. Most company negotiators insist on a strong no-strike clause as a price for entering an agreement. Spasmodic strikes over unresolved grievances also are undesirable from the union's point of view. While a few employees might be willing to engage in a long and bitter strike to obtain a satisfactory grievance settlement, most employees expect stable earnings during the term of the contract. Strikes over grievances are thus highly divisive for a union.

Despite obvious disadvantages to both sides, the use of strikes to enforce collective bargaining agreements is not totally obsolete. To the contrary, some agreements, particularly in the basic trades, have not included no-strike clauses and provide for no alternative method of dispute resolution other than a strike. Moreover, some agreements exempt certain sensitive areas from the coverage of both the arbitration and the no-strike clauses. However, approximately 95 percent of agreements provide for some form of dispute resolution as an alternative to the use of the strike.[4]

As reliance on strikes to enforce labor agreements became unacceptable, the parties began to turn to the courts for enforcement, with the nonbreaching party commencing a civil lawsuit against the breaching party. For years, a party that sought to use civil litigation to enforce a labor contract faced substantial procedural obstacles. Labor unions were at one time deemed unincorporated associations, and this sometimes necessitated service on individual members to commence a suit. On the other hand, if the union sought to enforce the rights of its members in court, there was the question of the real party since the members, not the union, were the beneficiaries of contract rights. The Taft-Hartley amendments to the National Labor Relations Act swept away these procedural obstacles to bringing suits under labor agreements. Section 301 of the Labor Management Relations Act provides that either party may maintain an action against the other in federal court for breach of a labor contract.

However, it is not feasible to wait for years to litigate some situations, such as whether the company promoted the wrong employee in derogation of another's seniority. Consequently, most agreements provide that unresolved grievances be submitted to arbitration for resolution. Such a provision, in many ways, closes the door to civil litigation against the company since the courts generally will insist that the aggrieved party utilize the agreed arbitration procedure. Thus, except in extraordinary circumstances, there is virtually no civil litigation against companies for breach of labor contracts.

Similarly, the right of the company to sue the union in court depends on how the parties define a grievance in the contract. That is, is a grievance a complaint by *either* the company or the union, or is a grievance simply a complaint made by the union or the employees against the company? If the agreement clearly permits the company to file a grievance and if it further provides for the arbitration of all unresolved grievances, the company also would be required to follow the agreed procedure. A likely situation in which the company might want to sue the union for breach of contract would be a violation of the no-strike clause. Although courts are slow and civil litigation is cumbersome, courts are more likely than arbitrators to award substantial damages against a union for such a violation. Therefore, company negotiators should consider carefully whether the company wants to waive its right to civil litigation by insisting on the right to arbitrate union breaches of the contract.

In summary, neither strikes nor civil litigation provides a satisfactory method of settling the day-by-day questions that arise under labor contracts. As a result, the vast majority of labor agreements provide for some form of binding arbitration. Although arbitration may have its drawbacks, a tremendous volume of decisions is being issued on a regular basis. Grievance arbitration has become an integral part of the American system of labor relations.

COURT RECOGNITION OF GRIEVANCE ARBITRATION

In the commercial world, arbitration has long been used as an alternative to litigation; for many years the courts tended to view grievance arbitration in a similar light. This view carried with it the standard narrow interpretation of the arbitration clause. Thus, employers who had doubts as to whether a certain dispute was arbitrable could, and frequently did, take advantage of the courts' restrictive view in either of two ways: (1) they might simply refuse to arbitrate in the first place or (2) if an arbitration were conducted, they might refuse to honor the award on the grounds that the arbitrator exceeded his or her jurisdiction. In either event, the union was forced into court, seeking either an order to arbitrate or an order to abide by the award.

In resolving such disputes, the courts would scrutinize the arbitration clause and the substantive provisions of the agreement to ensure that the dispute arose under and was governed by the express language of the contract. An examination of the language of a contract to determine its applicability to a particular grievance will more than likely lead to a consideration of the merits of the case. Under this procedure, the courts had the ultimate say as to contract interpretation; they frequently second-guessed arbitrators when deciding whether a party had to comply with an award.

The role of the courts with regard to grievance arbitration underwent a dramatic, sudden, and complete change. The stage was set for change in the courts' attitude toward grievance arbitration in 1947, when Congress passed the Taft-Hartley amendments to the National Labor Relations Act. In these amendments, Congress included section 203 (D), which states a preference for the method of dispute resolution agreed by the parties.[5] This amounted to nothing less than a congressional endorsement of arbitration and a recognition of the vital role of grievance arbitration under existing agreements in our system of labor relations. Section 203 (D) was not intended to deprive the National Labor Relations Board of its ultimate jurisdiction and authority with regard to unfair labor practices, as distinct from grievances alleging contractual violations.

Arbitration achieved ultimate victory in the courts in 1960, when the United States Supreme Court decided three cases: *United Steelworkers* v. *Warrior & Gulf Navigation Co.* 363 U.S. 574, 80 S. Ct. 1347 (1960); *United Steelworkers* v. *American Manufacturing Company*, 363 U.S. 564, 80 S. Ct. 1343 (1960); and *United Steelworkers* v. *Enterprise Wheel & Car Corp.*, 363 U.S. 593, 80 S. Ct. 1358 (1960). These decisions are commonly referred to as the *Steelworkers Trilogy*.

In the *Trilogy*, the Supreme Court recognized the crucial distinction between arbitration in the commercial world and grievance arbitration under a labor contract. In the commercial world, arbitration is a substitute for litigation; in labor relations, arbitration is primarily a substitute for strikes. Litigation never really provided a serious alternative for grievance resolution; hence a party that agreed to arbitrate was not really concerned about abandoning the safeguards of the legal system. The concern, however, was providing an alternative to strikes during the term of the agreement. Thus, in labor relations the quid pro quo that the employer receives in exchange for agreeing to be bound by an arbitrator's decision is the union's promise not to strike during the term of the agreement.

As a result, the Supreme Court recognized that a restrictive view of arbitration had no place in labor relations. Stated differently, in labor relations both parties receive a substantial benefit from the agreement to arbitrate; consequently arbitration provisions should be given a broad interpretation. The court adopted this approach when it held that, in construing a grievance arbitration clause, all doubt should be resolved in favor of arbitrability, particularly in those cases in which the agreement contained a broad no-strike clause. Students of labor relations should read each of the cases cited in detail, for they are rich in dicta, authoritative commentaries about the application of the law.

One of the cases, *Warrior & Gulf Navigation*, illustrates the sweep and impact of the *Trilogy* decisions. The employer was in the business of transporting steel and steel products by barge; it maintained a terminal at Chickasaw, Alabama, where it performed maintenance and repair work on its barges. Between 1956 and 1958 it laid off some employees, reducing the bargaining unit from 42 to 23 men. The reduction was in part attributable to the employer's contracting out, to other companies, work that had previously been done by its employees. The union filed a grievance in which it protested the contracting out of work; inasmuch as the matter remained unresolved, the union sought arbitration.

The labor agreement in effect included a broad arbitration clause that provided for the arbitration of disputes between the parties as to the meaning and application of the agreement. Arbitrability was limited, however, by a provision stating that "matters that are strictly a function of management shall not be subject to arbitration." The employer took the position that contracting out was strictly a function of management and therefore this dispute was expressly excluded from the coverage of the arbitration clause. The union's response was a suit in the United States district court in which the union asked that the employer be ordered to comply with the agreement to arbitrate.

In deciding whether to issue an order to arbitrate, the district court first had to determine if the agreement provided for the arbitration of this dispute, since the obligation to arbitrate is founded in the contract and a party can be compelled to arbitrate only what he had agreed to arbitrate. The obligation to arbitrate depended on whether contracting out was strictly a function of management. If so, it was expressly excluded from the coverage of the arbitration clause.

To determine whether contracting out fell within the exclusion, the district court examined the negotiating history of the parties and explored the parties' treatment of the subject. Clearly the court was considering the merits of the dispute, which went beyond arbitrability. Based on this evidence, the district court concluded that contracting out was a function of management and that the company's right to contract out was not limited by the agreement in any respect. Thus, the decision of the court was complete both as to the question of arbitrability and the question of merit. The United States court of appeals, in a divided vote, upheld the district court; it held that the collective agreement had withdrawn from the grievance procedure matters that were strictly a function of management and that contracting out was within that exception.

The United States Supreme Court reversed both the district court and the court of appeals. In its reversal, it acknowledged that when the district court was asked to order a reluctant party to arbitrate, it was forced to make an initial determination of arbitrability. However, in deciding whether the company had breached its agreement to arbitrate, the lower courts had applied the wrong criteria. The district court should have made a simple determination as to whether the agreement provided for the arbitration of this type of dispute. With regard to this determination, the Supreme Court said: "An order to arbitrate a particular grievance should not be denied unless it may be said *with positive assurance* that the arbitration clause is not susceptible to an interpretation that covers the asserted dispute. *Doubts should be resolved in favor of coverage.*" [Emphasis supplied.]

Concerning the scope of the exclusion for matters that were "strictly a function management," the Supreme Court suggested that the district court should have confined its inquiry to the face of the agreement and it should have avoided going deeper into the intent since such an inquiry naturally leads to a consideration of the merits. In this regard the Court said: "In the absence of any express provision excluding a particular grievance from arbitration, we think only the most forceful evidence of a purpose to exclude the claim from arbitration can prevail particularly where, as here, the exclusion clause is vague and the arbitration clause is quite broad." The Court followed with the caveat that any attempt to infer such a purpose under these facts would lead to a consideration of the merits, a matter within the province of the arbitrator.

It takes little effort to appreciate the tremendous significance of this portion of the decision. It would be impossible to determine positively, looking only at the face of the agreement, that the parties intended contracting out to be strictly a function of management. By leaving that determination to the arbitrator and confining itself to simple determination of whether the agreement provided for the arbitration of this type of dispute, the Supreme Court enhanced the role of the arbitrator and greatly limited the role of the courts in the interpretation of collective bargaining agreements. No longer would employers succeed when they refused to arbitrate unless the subject matter of the dispute was expressly, or at least plainly, excluded from the coverage of the arbitration clause.

Warrior & Gulf did far more than simply narrow the defense of nonarbitrability, however. It also set up a substantial roadblock for those who would refuse to comply with an arbitrator's award on the grounds that the arbitrator had exceeded his or her jurisdiction. Thus, another all too common avenue of defense was closed, or at least greatly restricted. Before this decision, if an arbitrator were to base an award on something other than the express language of the contract, such as past practice or the spirit of the agreement, the losing party might refuse to comply with the award on the grounds that the arbitrator had exceeded his or her authority. The basis for this argument was that the arbitrator's function was limited solely to interpreting the express terms of the agreement.

Here again, in deciding whether to order compliance with the award, the courts frequently would jump into the merits of the dispute. But in the portion of *Warrior & Gulf* devoted to dicta, the Supreme Court made some critical observations as to the nature of a labor agreement, the manner in which it might be interpreted, and the authority of the arbitrator.

> The collective bargaining agreement states the rights and duties of the parties. It is more than a contract; it is a generalized code to govern a myriad of cases which the draftsmen cannot wholly anticipate.... The collective agreement covers the whole employment relationship. It calls into being a new common law—the common law of a particular industry or of a particular plant.... The labor arbitrator's source of law is not confined to the express provisions of the contract, as the industrial common law—the practices of the industry and the shop—is equally a part of the collective bargaining agreement although not in it. The labor arbitrator is usually chosen because of the parties' confidence in his knowledge of the common law of the shop and their trust in his personal judgment to bring to bear considerations which are not expressed in the contract as criteria for judgment. The parties expect that his judgment of a particular grievance will reflect not only what the contract says but, insofar as the collective bargaining agreement permits, such factors as the effect upon productivity of a particular

result, its consequence to the morale of the shop, his judgment whether tensions will be heightened or diminished. For the parties' objective in using the arbitration process is primarily to further their common goal of uninterrupted production under the agreement, to make the agreement serve their specialized needs. The ablest judge cannot be expected to bring the same experience and competence to bear upon the determination of a grievance, because he cannot be similarly informed.

It takes little effort to appreciate the significance of these observations. The circumstances under which a losing party could complain because the arbitrator went beyond the express language of the contract in his considerations became quite limited. The court simply was saying what the arbitrator *might* consider, not what he or she *should* consider. Although the authority of the arbitrator became great, it is not without limits. In its decision in *Enterprise Wheel & Car Corp.*, also part of the *Trilogy*, the Court cautioned that while arbitrators may look for guidance from many sources, they do not sit to dispense their own brand of industrial justice and their awards are legitimate only so long as they draw their essence from the collective agreement. Thus, on a few occasions a court will find that the arbitrator exceeded his or her jurisdiction.

LEGISLATIVE AND JUDICIAL INCURSIONS

During the 1930s and 1940s a great deal of legislative and judicial attention was devoted to the process of collective bargaining. These subjects were of primary concern to Congress in 1935 when it enacted the Wagner Act (National Labor Relations Act). Many believe that by 1960 legislative emphasis seemed to shift from encouraging collective bargaining (or at least ensuring a free choice) to providing statutory, rather than privately negotiated, solutions to the nation's social problems. For example, Title VII of the Civil Rights Act of 1964 recognized that a successful employer and a comfortable union would not voluntarily give priority to the elimination of discrimination in the work environment. This is not to accuse unions and management of being naturally biased. But it is naive to believe that they would shove aside their primary interests in order to champion social progress. In any event, the 1960s and 1970s brought a literal avalanche of state and federal laws regulating the employment relationship. The more noteworthy statutes include the Equal Pay Act Amendments to the Fair Labor Standards Act (1963); Title VII of the Civil Rights Act of 1964; the Age Discrimination in Employment Act of 1967; the Occupational Safety and Health Act (1970); and the Employee Retirement Income Security Act (1974).

The responsibility for the interpretation and administration of statutes generally is assigned to administrative agencies. Appeals of their decisions and rulings invariably are presented in court. Arbitration simply has no role to play in this scheme. The result of this awesome amount of legislation is that the courts literally have been forced into concerning themselves with many everyday aspects of the employment relationship, such as safety, recruitment, and pay differentials that separate the sexes. Some professionals in the arbitration community are deeply concerned that the interference of the courts will bring about a decline in the role and finality of arbitration.

This concern was highlighted when the Supreme Court handed down the landmark decision of *Alexander v. Gardner-Denver Company* 415 U. S. 36, 94 S. Ct. 1011 (1974). On September 29, 1969, the Gardner-Denver Company discharged Harrell Alexander, Sr., a black employee, for the alleged offense of producing too many defective, unusable parts. The labor contract included a standard proper-cause criterion for discipline or discharge, a broad arbitration clause, and a clause providing no discrimination against any employee on account of race, color, religion, sex, national origin, or ancestry. The employee filed a grievance protesting the discharge.

During the processing of the grievance, the employer rejected all the employee's claims. The matter was scheduled to be heard in arbitration November 20, 1969. Before the hearing, the grievant filed a charge of racial discrimination with the Colorado Civil Rights Commission, which referred the complaint to the Equal Employment Opportunity Commission. At the November 20, 1969, arbitration hearing, the grievant testified that his discharge was the result of racial discrimination; he informed the arbitrator that he had filed a charge with the Colorado commission because he could not trust the union. On December 30, 1969, the arbitrator ruled that the grievant had been terminated for just cause. However, the decision did not refer specifically to the claim of racial discrimination. On July 25, 1970, the Equal Employment Opportunity Commission determined that there was not reasonable cause to believe that a violation of Title VII of the Civil Rights Act of 1964 occurred. Consequently, the terminated employee was notified of his right to institute a civil action in federal court within 30 days if he wished to pursue his Title VII claims on his own, despite the Equal Employment Opportunity Commission's determination.

The Supreme Court gave the following account of the somewhat unfriendly reception that the employee received in federal court when he availed himself of his right to sue:

> The District Court granted respondent's motion for summary judgment and dismissed the action. 346 F. Supp. 1012 (1971). The court found that the claim of racial discrimination had been submitted to the arbitrator and resolved adversely to petitioner. It then held that petitioner, having voluntarily elected to pursue his grievance to final arbitration under the nondiscrimination clause of the collective-bargaining agreement, was bound by the arbitral decision and thereby precluded from suing his employer under Title VII. The Court of Appeals for the Tenth Circuit affirmed *per curiam* on the basis of the District Court's opinion....

Certiorari was granted by the U. S. Supreme Court; to the horror of many in the labor relations community, the decision of the lower court was reversed. Implicit throughout the majority opinion is a recognition of the basic fact that statutory rights such as those conferred by Title VII and contractual rights created by a labor agreement are separate and distinct. The former are founded in legislation; the latter are based on the contractual undertakings of the parties.

In view of the fact that statutory and contractual rights stand on separate footings, the Supreme Court disagreed with the conclusion of the district court that the employee had forfeited his private cause of action by electing to pursue his claim in arbitration. In this regard, the Court said:

> That doctrine, which refers to situations where an individual pursues remedies that are legally or factually inconsistent, has no application in the present context. In submitting his grievance to arbitration, an employee seeks to vindicate his contractual right under a collective-bargaining agreement. By contrast, in filing a lawsuit under Title VII, an employee asserts independent statutory rights accorded by Congress. The distinctly separate nature of these contractual and statutory rights is not vitiated merely because both were violated as a result of the same factual occurrence. And certainly no inconsistency results from permitting both rights to be enforced in their respectively appropriate forums.

In addition, the Supreme Court was abundantly clear as to what it considered the appropriate forum for the enforcement of Title VII rights:

> Arbitral procedures, while well suited to the resolution of contractual disputes, make arbitration a comparatively inappropriate forum for the final resolution of rights created by Title VII. This conclusion rests first on the special role of the arbitrator, whose task is to effectuate the intent of the parties rather than the requirements of enacted legislation. Where the collective-bargaining agreement conflicts with Title VII, the arbitration must follow the agreement. To be sure, the tension between contractual and statutory objectives may be mitigated where a collective-bargaining agreement contains provisions facially similar to those of Title VII. But other facts may still render arbitral processes comparatively inferior to judicial processes in the protection of Title VII rights. Among these is the fact that the specialized competence of arbitrators pertains primarily to the law of the shop, not the law of the land.

Both the district court and the court of appeals were concerned that if an employee who had unsuccessfully pursued his or her claim in arbitration were permitted to litigate the same claim in a trial *de novo*, the employee would get "two bites at the apple." In the minds of many who strongly disagree with the Supreme Court's decision, the granting of the second bite jeopardized the finality of arbitration. But the Supreme Court was clear, recognizing no such concern or problem:

The District Court and the Court of Appeals reasoned that to permit an employee to have his claim considered in both the arbitral and judicial forums would be unfair since this would mean that the employer, but not the employee, was bound by the arbitral award. In the District Court's words, it could not "accept a philosophy which gives the employee two strings to his bow when the employer has only one...." This argument mistakes the effect of Title VII. Under the Steelworkers Trilogy, an arbitral decision is final and binding on the employer and employee, and judicial review is limited as to both. But in instituting an action under Title VII, the employee is not seeking review of the arbitrator's decision. Rather, he is asserting a statutory right independent of the arbitration process. An employer does not have "two strings to his bow" with respect to an arbitral decision for the simple reason that Title VII does not provide employers with a cause of action against employees. An employer cannot be the victim of discriminatory employment practices.

The procedure established by the Supreme Court in the *Gardner-Denver* case that applies to the enforcement of Title VII and other statutory rights stands in marked contrast to the policies adopted by the National Labor Relations Board. In *Spielberg Mfg. Co.*, 112 NLRB 1080 (1955) the board set forth certain standards and circumstances under which it would respect an arbitrator's decision. *Spielberg* applies to those cases in which the facts give rise to a contractual violation *and* an unfair labor practice. Moreover, the matter must have been heard in arbitration before an attempt to litigate the unfair labor practice. In *Collyer Insulated Wire*, 192 NLRB 837 (1971) the board went a step further and held that under certain circumstances it would defer to arbitration, that is, refuse to hear the case unless the parties first proceeded to arbitration. Thus, *Collyer* applies to those situations in which the case was brought to the board without first having been heard in arbitration. However, after having established *Collyer* deferral, the board partially retreated. In *General American Transp. Corp.*, 228 NLRB No. 2 (1977), Betty Murphy, who was then chairman, voted with two other members of the board to refuse to defer to arbitration in cases involving alleged discrimination against individual employees. Only time will tell whether the board will further restrict *Collyer* or abandon it totally. In any event, the applicability of both *Spielberg* and *Collyer* is limited to cases that involve the National Labor Relations Act (Labor Management Relations Act); neither affects the impact of *Gardner-Denver*, which applies to other statutory rights.

In summary, the message that the U.S. Supreme Court gave to arbitrators in *Gardner-Denver* is as clear and unmistakable as the message that it gave to the courts in *Warrior & Gulf Navigation Co.* In *Warrior & Gulf* the message to the courts is that in those situations in which disputes are included within the coverage of an arbitration clause, questions of contract interpretation and enforcement are within the province of the arbitrator. *Gardner-Denver* puts arbitrators on notice that the courts are the proper forum for the interpretation and enforcement of statutory rights and that employees shall have access to the courts regardless of prior arbitration. Thus, except for NLRB matters, the line of demarcation between arbitrators and the courts has become relatively clear.

Some characteristics inherent in the arbitration process clearly make it an unsuitable forum for statutory interpretation and enforcement. So long as the parties remain free to select any arbitrator and so long as arbitrators remain free to disregard precedent, arbitration will always lack consistency and predictability. This may not be fatal with regard to decisions that pertain to a specific agreement and that bind no one other than the parties. Statutes, on the other hand, apply to a broad spectrum of groups and individuals. Consistency is essential; there can be no real justice without it. Apparently the courts are more than willing to leave the task of contract interpretation and enforcement to arbitrators; most arbitrators are willing to return the compliment and leave statutory interpretation and enforcement to the courts.

How deeply will the courts become involved in labor relations? That will depend on the number and scope of the statutes that are enacted. During the Reagan administration, the trend toward increasing government regulations has come to a screeching halt. Many believe, however, that this is but a breathing spell before the flow of regulatory legislation resumes. If so, the courts inevitably will become even more involved. If the current trend continues, the responsibility for contract interpretation will remain with arbitrators; thus arbitration will remain an important aspect of resolving conflict between management and unions in the working world.

Much has been made of the so-called second bite of the apple that *Gardner-Denver* gives employees. Some see this as a grave peril to the finality of arbitration. But usually the parties themselves knowingly and willfully (perhaps for good reason) created the so-called first bite when they extracted language from a statute and included it in a labor agreement. It is the parties' privilege to create contractual obligations that parallel statutory obligations. By exercising this privilege, however, they should not be able to obliterate statutory rights that otherwise exist.

This is not to suggest that arbitrators should totally ignore the law. There certainly will be occasions when legal interpretations are relevant to contract interpretation. Suppose that a contract is ambiguous and that it could be construed in either of two ways. Further assume that one construction would be consistent with the law and the other inconsistent. Certainly the presumption is reasonable that the parties intended that the agreement be applied consistently with the law. However, in this situation, the arbitrator is considering the law only for the purpose of interpreting the agreement.

A second development of fairly recent origin that merits comment is the increase in the use of streamlined procedures to reduce the cost of grievance arbitration and to eliminate delays. An inherent characteristic of the arbitration process is that the parties not only select the arbitrator but also determine the conditions under which the arbitrator serves. For many years, both management and labor seemed reluctant to exercise their full discretion in determining specifically their arbitration procedures. Today, however, a trend toward considerable experimentation with various innovations designed to fit the specific needs of parties seems to be developing.

A notable example is expedited arbitration within the basic steel industry. Traditionally arbitration within some of the large steel companies has been conducted before boards of arbitration. At some point, the parties recognized that every grievance is not a matter of precedent and that all cases do not require full procedural treatment. The parties therefore established an expedited arbitration procedure for those cases. For example, discipline cases that present simple questions of fact and usually involve relatively short periods of suspension are likely candidates.

The arbitrators for these cases are selected on a rotation basis from a list of expedited arbitrators. This list is composed of individuals who have indicated that they are willing to serve and previously have been screened by the parties. An expedited arbitrator is paid a flat rate for each hearing day and receives no other compensation; he or she is not permitted to charge additional amounts for time spent in research or drafting decisions. The hearings are informal; briefs and transcripts are excluded. In a typical day, an expedited arbitrator will hear three or four cases. Decisions that must be mailed within 48 hours of the hearing are brief by desire of the parties and by necessity.

The use of expedited arbitration has spread far beyond the steel industry. Every day the list grows of organizations that have tailored some special form of arbitration to fit their specific needs. The American Arbitration Association has developed an expedited arbitration procedure available to their clients upon request.

Expedited arbitration has its critics, who insist that it reduces the number of settlements and increases the number of cases that are arbitrated. It has, on the other hand, received the enthusiastic endorsement of many who see it as a means of reducing the cost of arbitration and of avoiding large backlogs of pending cases. Regardless of the merits of the expedited process, it certainly provides a sound example of the parties assuming full control over the arbitration process. They have not only selected the arbitrators but also written the rules of the game. This trend is likely to continue; in the future, parties will no doubt exhibit even more imagination in tailoring arbitration procedures for their own purposes. Arbitration is, after all, a private system of jurisprudence that belongs to the parties.

The third trend is the possible use of arbitration as a final step in the dispute settlement process for nonunion employees. It perhaps would be more accurate to speak of this development as a prediction rather than a trend. Many nonunion employers voluntarily have adopted some form of grievance procedure. This may be done for various reasons, not the least of which may be a desire to remain nonunion. Few of these voluntary procedures include some form of binding arbitration as the final step for resolving grievances. This development seems most likely to occur in public or quasi-public institutions such as hospitals and educational organizations rather than in the typical nonorganized manufacturing plant. It is highly unlikely that most private businesses are ready to yield voluntarily to the discretion of an arbitrator.

There has been some legislative movement in this regard. Legislation introduced in a number of state legislatures would establish a just-cause standard for discharge of employees, especially including nonunion employees. It is not inconceivable that such a bill will be enacted. In its 1982 session, the International Labor Organization passed a resolution urging national governments to pass laws regulating the conditions for discharging employees.

Widespread adoption of such legislation in the near future, at least in the United States, seems highly unlikely. But should some legislative body seriously consider legislation that would statutorily impose a just-cause standard for the discharge of employees, serious caution and deliberation would be required. A moment's reflection suggests that the consideration of such legislation poses profoundly interesting questions, not the least of which is whether arbitration would be the appropriate form for enforcement and interpretation. Recall the Supreme Court's remarks in *Gardner-Denver* that arbitrators are experts in the law of the shop, not the law of the land. If such a just-cause standard is legislated, should there be some sort of administrative "referee" system for enforcement? Referees are used to enforce statutes governing unemployment insurance and workers' compensation, and the use of a referee system as an alternative to arbitration would circumvent many of the concerns expressed in *Gardner-Denver*.

The dicta set forth in the *Trilogy* are also relevant to these considerations. It was noted in the *Trilogy* that when the parties agree to arbitration, it is the arbitrator's decision, not the court's, that the parties have bargained for *(American Manufacturing Company)*. Leaving contract interpretation to arbitrators makes good sense when considered in this light. It is painfully apparent, however, that this logic would not apply to a statutorily imposed just-cause standard. When the parties have not bargained at all, would it be proper to impose arbitration in its present form? Due process and justice for legislatively secured rights would seem at least to require that some sort of appeal procedure be established. Aside from due process considerations, when statutes are involved, the need for consistency and predictability becomes critical. Unless the enforcement procedures under an arbitration process include a right of appeal, such consistency would be difficult to ensure.

Serious reflection on these matters will be required before the right of arbitration is extended via statute to nonunion employees. If arbitration is to be used in a statutory scheme, it will likely be in a totally different form than the current standard grievance arbitration process.

Reference Notes

[1] Elkouri, *How Arbitration Works*, 573.

[2] For a classic discussion of this concept, see Archibald Cox, "Reflections upon Labor Arbitration," *Harvard Law Review* 72 (1959): 1498-1499.

[3] *NLRB* v. *Acme Industrial Co.*, 385 U.S. 432 (1967).

[4] Lloyd G. Reynolds, *Labor Economics and Labor Relations*, 8th ed. (Englewood Cliffs, N.J.: Prentice-Hall, 1982), 409.

[5] 61 Stat. 154, 29 U.S.C. § 173 (d).

CHAPTER 6

Preparing for Arbitration

The following scenario could occur in any organization. A highly skilled employee with considerable experience was instructed by a young foreman to perform a task in a certain way. The employee believed that the foreman's approach was wrong and proceeded to do the job in his own way. Although the employee was ultimately successful, he did ignore his foreman's instructions with regard to procedure. The employer believed that authority (particularly that of the foreman) had been challenged; consequently, a 10-day disciplinary suspension for insubordination was issued. The union challenged the suspension in the grievance procedure. The matter became a cause célèbre among the rank and file since the foreman was intensely disliked. Moreover, the employee was proved correct with regard to procedure. Inasmuch as the parties were unable to resolve the matter, the union filed a timely appeal to arbitration.

THE APPEAL TO ARBITRATION

What is next on the agenda? In other words, what happens after a grievance has been transformed into a case pending arbitration. In a corporation it is quite likely that, on appeal, the file will be sent either to the corporate legal department or to outside counsel. A similar pattern is likely to be followed by the union; the file will be transmitted to house counsel or referred to a law firm. This is not to say that lawyers are always involved in the preparation and presentation of an arbitration case. Certainly many union officials, usually international representatives or business agents, are extremely competent and experienced advocates. In a similar vein, many management labor relations directors can more than hold their own in arbitration. However, lawyers often become involved at this stage of the proceedings.

When an attorney receives a file, he or she first examines it coldly from a single point of view: "Can I win this case in arbitration?" Far too often, this is the first truly objective examination of the case. Attorneys are usually far removed from the individuals involved. It would be most unlikely that the corporate attorney would have regular contact with the foreman in the scenario; the union attorney would not be exposed to daily ear beatings from the rank and file. Thus, in the quiet of their offices, the lawyers can evaluate the case in a pressure-free atmosphere. Assuming that the attorneys have some expertise in labor relations, they will concentrate on critical issues and avoid being sidetracked by irrelevancies. By way of illustration, the insubordination case might turn on two critical points: (1) Did the foreman give a clear, direct, and unequivocal order? (2) Did the grievant, by words or actions, demonstrate a willful intent to disobey? Factors such as the unpopularity of the foreman, the popularity of the employee, and the correctness of the employee's action will be considered irrelevant.

Cases that reach an attorney have been fairly well screened during the final stages of the grievance procedure since the parties' representatives usually have sufficient sophistication to select critical issues. However, some cases with obvious and fatal flaws slip through the grievance procedure without being recognized as hopeless or, at best, poor bets. Moreover, objective consideration sometimes is hindered during the initial processing of a grievance by familiarity with the individuals involved or by internal pressures. What happens in such a situation? Does the fact that a case has been appealed to arbitration mean that all further negotiations are precluded? The answer is emphatically *no*; many cases appealed to arbitration are settled at some point short of receiving an arbitrator's decision.

Aside from the discovery of a fatal flaw, a variety of circumstances might prompt a party to initiate settlement discussions. The foreman in our scenario might terminate his employment, and his departure might remove internal pressure that hindered settlement. Although postappeal settlement negotiations are frequently initiated, there is some difference of opinion as to how this should be accomplished. Attorneys love to negotiate, particularly with other attorneys; if given a free reign, the result may be the creation of another informal step of the grievance procedure that follows the appeal to arbitration. The obvious danger is that the role of the grievance representatives may be undercut if attorneys take charge of postappeal settlement efforts. To avoid this, some organizations insist that labor relations representatives make all overtures toward settlement, regardless of whether a case has been appealed to arbitration, and further require that such overtures be made to the representatives' counterparts. Such a practice not only limits the attorneys' choice but also loses sight of the fact that lawyers frequently do an excellent job of working things out, particularly with other lawyers. So long as there are some clear-cut understandings to preserve internal harmony, it doesn't matter who settles a case.

After the file has been reviewed by whoever will serve as the parties' advocates, the next item on the agenda is selecting an arbitrator and scheduling a hearing. Well-drafted labor agreements invariably include some procedure for arbitrator selection. The following is a fairly typical provision:

> Unless the parties agree otherwise, the party who appealed the case to arbitration will request that the American Arbitration Association (or the Federal Mediation and Conciliation Service) furnish a list that includes the names of three arbitrators. The union will strike one name from the list, the company will strike a second, and the arbitrator who remains will be the designated arbitrator.

Particularly when arbitration is relatively infrequent for the parties, this type of selection procedure works reasonably well. Both the American Arbitration Association and the Federal Mediation and Conciliation Service maintain extensive rosters of experienced and qualified arbitrators whose qualifications have been thoroughly screened. A list containing a designated number of names can be readily obtained from either source. At least one mutually satisfactory arbitrator probably will be included when a list of three, five, or seven names is requested. The parties' familiarity with the arbitrators included on the list will depend on the frequency of arbitration.

When unfamiliar names are included on a requested list, there are several ways for a party to verify an arbitrator before selecting. Several publishers have services that report arbitration decisions; it is usually possible to read the decisions of a certain arbitrator. However, the majority of arbitration decisions are not published. Consequently a study of an arbitrator's previous awards will be incomplete at best. Some of the services that publish awards also include arbitrators' biographical sketches. Computerized data services providing statistics on a given arbitrator's rulings on certain issues are available. Probably the most common method of researching an arbitrator is simply to contact associates in other firms or unions, who are usually more than willing to relate their experience with a certain arbitrator. In some industries and unions, decisions are circulated, and information of this type is exchanged as a matter of course.

When the parties arbitrate with some frequency (perhaps 10 or 15 cases per year), they probably will dispense with the formality of obtaining a list for every case. If four or five arbitrators are mutually satisfactory, they will simply rotate cases among that group by informal agreement. Since there is no commitment to any particular arbitrator, it is painless to drop an arbitrator from the rotation if either party becomes disenchanted. Moreover, if either party wants to discontinue the rotation, the parties may always turn to the procedure provided in the contract. In effect, all the parties have done is mutually agree to shortcut the procedure; as long as both parties are satisfied, they can select any arbitrator whom they wish without assistance from any outside organization or agency. Contract selection procedures should be drafted to permit this kind of flexibility. In other words, the use of lists should be mandated only when the parties do not agree on the selection.

What has been discussed so far is ad hoc arbitration, in which a particular arbitrator is selected to hear a specific case or group of cases. There are, of course, advantages and disadvantages to this type of arrangement. Ad hoc arbitrators who have no permanent relationship with the parties are believed less likely to attempt to mediate a dispute than permanent arbitrators. There may be some disagreement as to whether this is a positive or a negative attribute. Consistency and predictability likely suffer because the contract will be interpreted by several arbitrators, all with their own prejudices. Probably the greatest drawback to ad hoc arbitration, however, is no guarantee of the availability of arbitrators when needed because most arbitrators have extremely busy workloads and schedule hearings months in advance.

Many employers and unions prefer the use of a permanent arbitrator over ad hoc arbitration. Under this procedure, the parties mutually select a permanent arbitrator to hear their disputes. Inasmuch as the permanent arbitrator can reserve time within his or her schedule for the parties, this system eases the availability problem. Moreover, some gain would be expected in consistency and predictability since the parties will soon become familiar with their arbitrator's particular prejudices. A final benefit is that a permanent arbitrator is in an excellent position to win the confidence of the parties and may be able to contribute to their relationship by diplomatically providing constructive guidance when appropriate. It is a mistake, however, to believe that permanent arbitrators are in fact permanent. The relationship is terminable at the will of either party. It is often said that there is nothing less permanent than a permanent arbitrator.

Because arbitration is a private system of dispute resolution that leaves the parties free to tailor a procedure to fit their needs, many other variations have been devised. Particularly when arbitration occurs with some frequency, there is no simple formula to determine whether certain parties should rely on ad hoc arbitration, appoint a permanent arbitrator, use a tripartite panel, or establish a board. But the matter is of sufficient significance to merit considerable thought and attention.

SCHEDULING THE HEARING

It is customary to request that when notified of his/her appointment, the selected arbitrator furnish dates on availability to conduct a hearing. Better-known arbitrators often schedule hearings three or four months in advance. Several months may elapse after the arbitrator's selection before the case is heard. For the reasons explained later, several more months may pass after the hearing before a decision. It is unanimously agreed that time lags of six or seven months are intolerable and that the process must be hastened. If the employee in the scenario had been discharged rather than suspended, in all likelihood he would be without a source of income while awaiting an arbitrator's verdict. Delay also penalizes the employer since potential monetary damages continue to accrue and, in a case involving a discharge, frequently exceed a half year in back wages. In complex cases that involve several employees, potential damages in lost wages may rapidly approach the hundred thousand dollar mark.

The main solution that critics of the arbitration process advocate to eliminate delay is increasing the number of available arbitrators. To accomplish this, the American Arbitration Association and the Federal Mediation and Conciliation Service on occasion have cooperated with leading universities to conduct arbitrator training courses. At best, increasing the number of arbitrators is only a partial solution; it is probably directed at an aspect of the problem that the parties themselves have the power to abet. Many factors other than the alleged shortage of arbitrators contribute to delay. Moreover, while well-known arbitrators are in extreme demand, the vast majority of cases are given to a small percentage of arbitrators. There is certainly no shortage of individuals who want to arbitrate; many young, competent arbitrators are in the process of entering the field. The parties could do a great deal to alleviate the shortage by simply giving some of these aspiring but less prominent arbitrators a chance, particularly on cases that do not concern critical precedents. The 10-day suspension in the scenario presents issues of fact; did the foreman give a direct and unequivocal order and did the employee demonstrate a willful and deliberate intent to disobey? This case would be an ideal candidate for assignment to a young arbitrator. Many such individuals could schedule an immediate hearing and would undoubtedly be willing to issue a prompt decision.

Attention should also be given to factors that contribute to delay, other than the workload of arbitrators. Foremost in this regard, arbitrators are not the only individuals who have full schedules. Competent labor attorneys are unbelievably busy. The problem of scheduling a hearing is compounded in situations in which both parties are represented by counsel since a single date that is satisfactory to three busy individuals must be agreed. Other matters that cause delay may include the parties' insistence on a full scale hearing, which includes transcripts and briefs. At least three weeks should be allowed for the preparation of a transcript; the attorneys usually want a like amount of time after the receipt of the transcript in order to file briefs. Consequently two months will elapse after the hearing before the arbitrator can even begin to draft a decision.

In summary, if the parties in the scenario follow the usual pattern, that is, if they select a prominent arbitrator, both are represented by counsel, and they have a full-blown hearing with all the trimmings including transcripts and briefs, they can reasonably anticipate a time lag of at least six months after the arbitrator is selected before they will receive a decision.

If this is not tolerable, it is within their power to consider the many available options, such as dispensing with the transcript, to reduce the delay.

INVESTIGATING AND RESEARCHING THE CASE

Ordinarily, a considerable amount of investigation and research will be done by a party's representatives while the matter is being processed through the grievance procedure. Investigation and research in anticipation of arbitration, however, must usually go one step beyond what has already been accomplished. In the grievance procedure, a great deal of time and effort is devoted simply to ascertaining the facts—what actually happened. Collecting facts is the first step for an advocate; then he or she must always be concerned with questions of proof. It is one thing to know that something is true and quite another to prove it. A union might know that a practice is in effect under which overtime is always offered to the senior available employee; it might assert this practice during the processing of a grievance. In arbitration, however, a simple claim that a practice exists is not sufficient. A competent advocate would check the records and ascertain how many times overtime was worked and to whom it was offered during a given period. He or she would then carefully prepare an exhibit, summarize the findings, and ensure that he or she was able to lay a foundation for its admission. Suppose that the exhibit shows that overtime was worked on 92 occasions during the last two years and that without exception it was offered to the senior available employee. This would be clear and convincing proof of an unbroken practice. Painstaking investigation of this type wins arbitrations and distinguishes the competent and experienced advocate.

Since each arbitration case is unique to some degree, there is no magic formula for investigation and research that will always be satisfactory. The following is therefore simply a suggested starting point. To some degree, it has been arranged in order of persuasiveness; that is, the initial items probably have the most probative value. This does not mean, however, that the last items should be ignored; every item requires consideration.

1. Express Language of the Contract

The general issue that an arbitrator usually must resolve is, Did the employer violate the agreement? Hence, a starting point in all cases is to examine carefully the language of all relevant contract provisions. A party that intends to buck clear and express language faces a difficult task at best. If the agreement provides that seniority shall apply to layoff and recall but not to promotion, it is certainly going to be difficult for a union to represent a senior employee who was not promoted.

2. Prior Arbitration Decisions between the Same Parties

If an arbitrator previously interpreted a clause of an agreement in a certain way and if the parties included that clause without change in subsequent agreements, a strong argument can be that the prior arbitration decision became a part of the agreement. The basis for the argument is that if the parties did not agree with the prior decision, they could have changed the language. Hopefully the parties will have a system for indexing and locating prior decisions; this research should be done long before the appeal to arbitration is filed. The advocate should certainly verify the research. Nothing is more embarrassing than to learn in arbitration that the issue to be presented has been the subject of several prior cases, all decided by prominent arbitrators, and that none of the prior decisions support the advocate's position.

3. Past Practices of the Parties

There are two common and legitimate reasons why a party may argue past practice during an arbitration hearing: to give definition to an ambiguous term and to fill in a gap where the agreement is silent. When the agreement is ambiguous but not silent, if a party can prove that for years the ambiguous term has always been applied in a certain way, it is reasonable to assume that the parties intended the term to have a meaning consistent with their own practice. Assume that an agreement provides that employees who are assigned to jobs other than their regular job shall not suffer a loss of earnings as a result but shall be paid at the highest rate applicable either to their regular or temporary job. Suppose further that an employee has worked on four jobs during a given week. What is the regular job? If it can be established that without exception the first assignment during the week has been treated as the regular job, an ambiguous term has been given meaning.

A second and distinctly different purpose for making a past practice argument is a situation in which the agreement is not ambiguous but silent regarding a matter in issue. Most arbitrators no longer subscribe to the so-called reserved rights theory of interpreting a labor contract. They reject the argument that since at one time all rights were vested in management, they remain with management unless expressly limited by the agreement. To a large degree, this logic has been replaced by the belief that when a union executes an agreement and waives the right to strike during its term, there is an implied understanding that certain conditions, particularly benefits, in effect when the agreement was signed would remain in effect during the contract term. This is not to say that everything is fixed by practice. Because there has never been a layoff does not mean that there never will be. In a similar vein, the fact that a wheelbarrow has been used to move material does not preclude the subsequent purchase of a forklift truck. Preparing a past practice argument to fill a gap in the agreement is a time-consuming and arduous process. At a minimum, attention should be devoted to each of the following:

a) Carefully define the practice that is being established. For example, is an attempt being made to show that employees have a right to drink coffee, or a right both to drink and prepare it?

b) Make certain that the matter in issue falls within the category of subjects that are fixed by practice.

c) Establish a long and continued response to a given set of circumstances. A few isolated instances do not give rise to a reasonable expectation that a practice will be continued.

d) Prove that both parties were aware of the response and knowingly continued it. Undetected abuses of a privilege do not establish a binding practice.

4. Prior Arbitration Decisions within the Same Industry

It is often said that although arbitrators are not bound to follow precedent, they are certainly persuaded by it. This will be particularly true in rare instances in which the parties are confronted with an issue for the first time, the agreement is either silent or ambiguous, and no consistent practice exists. In such a situation, a decision by another arbitrator who ruled on a similar issue at another company within the same industry, may be persuasive.

5. Other Arbitration Decisions

Because of the vast number of arbitration cases that are decided and the large number of arbitrators involved, if an advocate looks long and hard enough, he or she can usually find some precedent to support almost any position. Simply because some arbitrator in another industry ruled in a certain way, the precedent need not be followed. However, precedent outside the industry should not be ignored. To the contrary, it may be helpful to introduce such a decision provided it is directly to the point, well-reasoned, and written by a known arbitrator. Sometimes gold is struck during the search for such decisions in the form of a prior decision by the arbitrator handling the present dispute. In that case, the precedential value takes on a new dimension.

As a caveat, even though the preceding suggestions to some degree have been arranged in order of persuasive value, proper research requires that some attention be given to all the categories. An advocate must never lose sight of the fact that he or she has two objectives when presenting a case in arbitration. The first is to persuade the arbitrator. The second is to give the arbitrator the ammunition needed to justify the award and explain the loss to the unsuccessful party.

It is impossible to stress adequately the need for taking the time to prepare for the actual presentation of the case. Competent advocates realize this and enter a hearing prepared to the hilt; their presentations are invariably well organized and convincing. Unfortunately all spokesmen in arbitration are not competent. An all too familiar scene occurs on the morning of the hearing in the dining room of the motel in which the hearing room is located. A party's spokesperson has arranged a last-minute breakfast meeting, frequently with witnesses that he or she is meeting for the first time. The spokesperson is desperately trying to put the case together, over bacon and eggs, shortly before the hearing is scheduled to begin. Although breakfast meetings are excellent to tie down last-minute details, it is absolutely foolhardy to attempt to organize an entire presentation on the morning of the hearing. The result of such haphazard preparation is invariably total disaster: the party's own witnesses are more deadly to their side than the opponent's; unplanned cross-examination devastates the examiner, not the witness; the closing statement is completely impromptu and rambling.

No matter how strong or righteous the merits of a case may be, it is essential to prevail during the hearing. An arbitrator is placed in a terrible position when the equities of the case favor the party that has done a miserable job of presentation. How can an arbitrator explain to the party who appeared to win during the hearing that it lost the case? Thus, each presentation must be thoroughly prepared; there is no substitute for hard work. Witnesses must be thoroughly interviewed. Tentative opening and closing statements should be drafted, exhibits prepared, documents organized, and a strategy for each cross-examination developed. To do less is a sure sign of inexperience and incompetence; preparation invariably distinguishes the truly competent advocate.

PART II

GRIEVANCE CASE SIMULATIONS

Donald S. McPherson
Kevin N. Rogers

Roles

UNION	MANAGEMENT
Grievant	Foreman
Chief Steward	Personnel Director

Role of the Grievant

Your name is Gary Stahl. You have been employed by the Willow Creek Foundry since 1965. You served one tour of duty in the Army from 1968 to 1970 and later returned to Willow Creek without loss of accumulated seniority and benefits. After performing a number of jobs, you are an apprentice pattern maker in a formal training program that has seven more months to run. After such considerable work experience, you find the routine work of the apprenticeship program unrewarding; the length of the program makes your boredom all the more discouraging.

In recent years you've had some problems at work. In July 1979 you walked off the job with three hours left on your shift, stayed home the next day, and failed to report the absence. You received a letter of reprimand. From late 1979 through 1980, you were absent from work on 18 occasions, reporting in sick less than half the time. Jim Mock, the foreman, tried to talk with you about the excessive absenteeism problem but you found that you had little in the way of explanation to offer. On March 3, 1980, you received a second letter of reprimand for excessive absenteeism.

You took extended medical leave of 20 days in September 1980 and again took an extended medical leave of 30 days in January 1981. You were diagnosed by a counseling psychologist as suffering from post Vietnam stress disorder, a fact that you find embarrassing. You served honorably and never asked for any favors. In your mind, this sounds like an excuse. Besides, you're not at all sure that you do have "it," despite what the psychologist said—whatever "it" is.

Following your additional unexcused absences (four) in April 1981, Jim Mock again discussed the problem with you, but you did not tell him of your condition. The psychologist is willing to provide documentation of his diagnosis at any time. You still see him occasionally, though you're not sure why you go or whether it does any good. In any case, you're keeping the "illness" to yourself, afraid that people, including your supervisors, may think that you're "nuts." When you had no satisfactory explanation for the April absences, Mock suspended you for three days.

In June and July 1981 you missed 11 days, and were suspended for a week, and given a final discharge warning. Then things seemed to fall into place for awhile; you weren't absent any more than anyone else. Lately, though, things seem to be falling apart; in the last month, you've missed 6 days. Mock told you today that you were to be discharged.

You contacted Jerry Held, your shop steward and an old buddy. He said that he'd report to Chief Steward Charlie Foster and that you should see Foster to fill him in on the details for your grievance. He urged you to tell Foster about the psychological problems and to reveal them to management. Otherwise, he said, the discharge will probably stick.

Role of the Chief Steward

Your name is Charlie Foster. You are chief steward of the union representing production employees of the Willow Creek Foundry. Earlier today, you received the following note from Jerry Held, the shop steward in the pattern shop.

> Charlie—
>
> Gary Stahl, an apprentice in the Pattern Shop, has received notification from Foreman Jim Mock that he is going to be discharged for chronic absenteeism.
>
> Gary has been with the company since 1965 and has served a tour of duty with the Army, during which time he maintained his seniority. He lost 9 days in 1979, 10 days in 1980, and 15 days in 1981. He had 20 days of medical leave in 1980 and 30 days in 1981. Of all the absences other than the medical leaves, he called in sick only six times. In the past month he missed 6 days. He has two written reprimands, a 3-day suspension, and a 5-day suspension for absenteeism.
>
> Needless to say, his record is not good. But Gary suffers from a medical condition known as post-Vietnam stress syndrome. I know this only because we go back a long way as friends—he can get documents from psychologists to prove the diagnosis but is refusing to use the condition as "an excuse." He seems embarrassed by it, afraid that people will think he's crazy.
>
> I think the company should be made aware of the problem before it takes the action. I've urged him to talk candidly with you—he wants to grieve—and told him that his only chance is to reveal his condition to management. With his seniority, he deserves another chance.
>
> His apprenticeship will be over in seven months and I think that he'll stop losing days when he moves to a permanent new position. He's always worked hard and well. I also suggest we urge the company to provide counseling for him—and others if they need it.
>
> Jerry

Role of the Foreman

Your name is Jim Mock. You have been a foreman since 1975 at the Willow Creek Foundry. You like your work and get along well with most of the employees.

Your biggest, or at least most difficult, problem is with Gary Stahl, a pattern shop apprentice who has been with the company since 1965. From

1968 to 1970 he served in the Army in Vietnam without loss of company seniority. Since 1979 Stahl has had an excessive number of absences although prior to that time he had been relatively regular in coming to work. He's a nice guy; his work, when he's there, is entirely satisfactory.

You've tried to speak with him on several occasions, but he seemed unable to provide any satisfactory explanations for his behavior. He has taken two extended medical leaves. For awhile, the problem seemed to be lessening, but it has recently cropped up again.

You've given Stahl two written reprimands for absenteeism, one in July 1979 and the second in March 1980. He was suspended for three days in April 1981 after 4 unexcused absences and for a week after 11 additional absences in June and July 1981. Last month he missed six days. You've recommended to David Keim, the personnel director, that he be discharged. Keim told you to notify him and then to fill him in completely before the formal action is taken.

You have nothing personal against Stahl, but you do have to get the work done and cannot with an absent employee. Under any notion of progressive discipline, you believe that discharge is warranted and, practically speaking, is the only measure left to take. When you notified Stahl, he said that he'd file a grievance.

You've prepared a summary of Stahl's record from his personnel file for Keim and have an appointment to see him.

Role of the Personnel Director

Your name is David Keim. You are personnel director of the Willow Creek Foundry. Yesterday one of the foremen, Jim Mock in the pattern shop, discussed a case of absenteeism involving one of the apprentices, Gary Stahl. He recommended discharge. In light of what he told you, you agreed, at least to the extent that you told him to notify the employee of the company's intent. You then asked Mock to fill you in completely.

Your secretary just brought in the following message with a note that Mock will be seeing you right after lunch:

Mr. Keim:

I have checked the personnel file of Gary Stahl, the problem employee whom we discussed. I think that you'll find the discharge recommendation justified based on this summary.

Absence Record

1979	9	
1980	10	called in sick only 6 times
1981	15	

Discipline Record for Absence

Written reprimand	July 1979
Written reprimand	March 1980

3-day suspension   April 1981
5-day suspension   June 1981

Stahl had six unexcused absences last month.

I have nothing against him. I have tried to talk with him numerous times, but he has no explanation. It seems that he isn't dealing with the problem. He had 50 days of extended medical leave in 1980 and 1981; I do think that he has some kind of problem. But we're not a social service agency, and I don't see how we can be expected to go further with him than we already have.

James Mock

Roles

UNION   MANAGEMENT

Grievant   Supervisor
Chief Steward   Personnel Director

Role of the Grievant

Your name is Ray Carter. You have worked for the KLM Standard Company in the pipe-fabricating department for five years. KLM is a tubular products company. Depending upon the order, you work at machines that bend pipes, thread them, and cut them to length—everything from four inches in length and only one-half inch in diameter to five feet in length and one foot in diameter. On March 11, while working a threading machine on an order of nine-inch pipe, you suffered an injury to your back. The machine jammed and twisted the pipe suddenly while you were readjusting the pipe's position. It threw you to the floor, not hard, but in such a way that you twisted severely in trying to keep your balance. You sought treatment in the dispensary and have been seeing your family doctor since the accident. For some time you've had fairly constant lower back pain, which was bearable, but recently you've developed shooting pains down the backs of your legs. Your doctor suggested that you see an orthopedic specialist.

On May 5 you saw the specialist, who diagnosed your problem as an injury to the lumbar region, accompanied by an inflammation of the sciatic nerves. The doctor said that your back injury itself was not serious and the sciatic problem could be cleared up, but not if you continued working. He said that you would need complete bed rest for at least one week, maybe as long as two or three weeks. He further urged that you go into the hospital where the bed rest could be enforced rigidly, he could monitor your progress, and you could take advantage of the physical therapy facilities. Reluctantly you agreed. He wrote a recommendation for you to take to work requesting an initial 10-day medical leave.

You took the letter to the company doctor at the dispensary, who approved it, pending approval from personnel. The personnel director, Walter Mishler, also approved a 10-day leave, beginning May 7. He emphasized strongly that you had to bring an official release from the orthopedist in order to return to work. When you finished the paperwork in the office, one of the clerks also reminded you not to return without the release form.

On May 13 the orthopedist examined you thoroughly in the hospital and said that it looked like you'd have to stay another week to 10 days. You were disappointed, but since the pain had lessened, you felt that you had no choice. On May 16 your wife brought to the hospital the following memo, which had been received in the mail that day at your home.

Date: May 15

Re: Sick Leave
To: R.Carter
From: Personnel Department

According to our records, your medical leave is about to expire. This is sent as a reminder that company policy requires a release form from your doctor before you can return to work. Please do not return without the form as you will not be permitted to return to work.

You should report to the Personnel Office with the doctor's release form at the time of your return to work. Please call if you have any questions.

On May 20 the orthopedist released you from the hospital and gave you a form saying that you could return to work effective May 23. You went into the plant today, May 23, reporting first to your supervisor, Ruth Billick, to tell her that you had returned and would take the paperwork to personnel. To your surprise, she said, "Don't bother changing; you don't work here anymore." She said that you failed to call in after being absent beyond the ending date of your leave for more than three consecutive days, and so the company considers it a voluntary resignation. Enraged, you demanded to be reinstated, pointing out that the contract says that no one can be discharged for a work-related injury and that you weren't released by your doctor. She said that you'd better take it up with personnel. You told her that you'd see your steward, Dick Mazey, to file a grievance immediately. You called him at his work station to fill him in briefly; he asked to see you over the lunch hour to provide details.

Role of the Steward

Your name is Richard Mazey. You are a shop steward, and chief steward, of the union representing employees at KLM Standard Company, a tubular products concern. You just got an incredible call from Ray Carter, a pipe fabricator. He wants to file a grievance over his discharge.

From what you could get over the phone, Carter suffered a work-related back injury some time ago. Several weeks ago, he applied for and received a 10-day medical leave to go into the hospital for treatment. He said that he was told by personnel not to return without a release form from his doctor. The doctor did not release him after 10 days; he actually stayed in the hospital for two weeks, until May 21. The doctor then gave him a clearance form for returning today, Monday, May 23. Carter said that when he returned, he was told that the company considered him a voluntary quit because he violated article 24 of the contract. You made an appointment to see him over the lunch hour and called the personnel office to leave a message that you wanted to talk with the director, Walter Mishler, about Carter's discharge as soon as possible.

Technically it appears that Carter violated the contract article. It certainly would have been sensible for him to call in. But you think that the company waived its right to that expectation by emphasizing to him not to return without a release from his doctor. Much more important, as you told Mishler's secretary to point out to him, article 39 of the contract prohibits the discharge of any employee for industrial illness or accident suffered on company property unless there is no work available for which the employee is qualified.

You still have to get the details from Carter, but it looks like a good grievance.

Role of the Supervisor

Your name is Ruth Billick. You are employed as a supervisor for the KLM Standard Company, a tubular products concern. One of the pipe fabricators in your department, Ray Carter, suffered a work-related back injury in March when a pipe threader malfunctioned and he was twisted awkwardly to the floor. He complained of back pain and leg pain since the accident.

On May 6 you were informed by the personnel office that Carter had been approved for a 10-day medical leave beginning May 7. As usual, you were the last to find out in such matters. You had to scramble to redo the work schedule. But you were glad that Carter was finally going to have his back cared for.

On May 18 the day that you expected Carter to return, he did not come to work, which caused more problems because you had him scheduled. You tried to call him at home all day but got no answer. At the end of the shift, you reported to personnel that he hadn't returned; the clerk told you that they had sent him a letter reminding him that his leave was about to end. The clerk said that the letter was mailed May 15.

Carter did not show up May 19 or 20. You continued trying to call but got no answer. On May 21 you went to see Walter Mishler, the personnel director, to discuss the matter. The two of you agreed that apparently Carter would have to be considered a voluntary quit according to article 24 of the contract. Since it was Saturday, Mishler said that he'd write a letter to Carter advising him of his termination on Monday, May 23.

Today, May 23, Carter showed up. You told him that he had voluntarily quit since he hadn't reported off. He blew up and demanded to be reinstated. You told him that he'd have to take it up with personnel. He left in a huff, saying that he was going to see Dick Mazey, the steward, to file a grievance.

Role of the Personnel Director

Your name is Walter Mishler, personnel director for KLM Standard Company, a tubular products manufacturer. You just got a message from your secretary that the union chief steward, Dick Mazey, wants to talk with you as soon as possible "about Ray Carter's discharge" and asks you to look at article 39 of the contract.

You called in your secretary and asked her to check with one of the clerks about Carter's status. The clerk reported that Carter had returned for work today, May 23, and was told by his supervisor, Ruth Billick, that he was considered a voluntary quit in violation of article 24. You told the clerk that the information confirmed your understanding.

In fact, you and Billick had discussed Carter's case the day before yesterday, Saturday, May 21, and agreed that you had no choice but to assume that he had voluntarily resigned. You told Billick that you'd write Carter a letter to that effect today. You asked your secretary for his file to review it.

Carter was granted a 10-day medical leave effective May 7 for treatment for a work-related back injury suffered March 11. He completed all the required paperwork. You recall telling him specifically that he'd have to get clearance from his doctor before he returned at the end of his leave. Billick reported that Carter had not shown up for work May 18, when he was scheduled to return, or May 19 or 20. When you and she talked May 21, she told you that she had tried to call him each day without success.

Also in his file is a copy of the standard reminder form sent to employees near the end of any scheduled medical leaves.

Date: May 15

RE: Sick Leave
To: R. Carter
From: Personnel Department

According to our records, your medical leave is about to expire. This is sent as a reminder that company policy requires a release form from your doctor before you can return to work. Please do not return without the form as you will not be permitted to return to work.

You should report to the Personnel Office with the doctor's release form at the time of your return to work. Please call if you have any questions.

It seems fairly clear to you. Carter knew when his leave was up and the office even sent him a reminder. As a five-year employee, he also knew full well that he was required to report in if he were going to be absent from work—or at least he should have known, because it's in the contract. He was not discharged; he voluntarily quit.

You'll want to review everything with Billick before meeting with the union steward.

Other Relevant Information

ARTICLE 24

....Unless caused by circumstances beyond the control of the employee, absence from work for three consecutive working days without notifying the company will be considered a voluntary resignation.

ARTICLE 39

....As long as work for which the employee is qualified is available, no employee shall be discharged on account of an industrial illness or injury suffered on company property.

Case 2: An Extended Illness

Roles

UNION	MANAGEMENT

UNION

Grievant
A New Shop Steward
Chief Shop Steward

MANAGEMENT

Housekeeping Supervisor
Manager, Labor Relations

Background

On April 5 Housekeeping Supervisor Janice Sheldon asked Lyla Brown, a custodian, to remain at the end of the shift and work overtime. Brown said that she could not work overtime that night because of a prior commitment and suggested that other, more junior, custodians be asked. The supervisor agreed, recognizing both Brown's seniority and her reason as valid.

About 15 minutes later, the supervisor brought a work sheet for April 5 with *refused overtime* marked beside Brown's name and asked her to initial the sheet next to her name. Thinking that the work sheet might go into her personnel record as a bad mark, Brown refused to initial it, responding that she had refused overtime assignments in the past and never had been asked to initial a work sheet.

Supervisor Sheldon replied that employees frequently had been asked to initial overtime refusals and that she was simply making the procedure standard. She explained that the work sheets were used only as a record to show that the company had offered overtime to employees in accordance with the contract.

Lyla Brown did not particularly like Sheldon, who had a reputation among the custodial crew as being sneaky because of how she checked on employees to be sure that work was being done properly. Believing she was being tricked, Brown continued to refuse to initial the work sheet and said that she would testify at any time that she had turned down the overtime. Supervisor Sheldon then gave Brown a clear and direct order to initial the work sheet and told her she would be insubordinate and liable to disciplinary action if she refused.

Brown, a recently elected shop steward, then asked if she could call over another shop committee member at a nearby work station. The supervisor agreed. Asking the other steward to serve as a witness, Brown then repeated that she was officially declining the overtime for the record, but said she would not initial the work sheet unless the supervisor could show some rule requiring employees to do so.

Supervisor Sheldon then explained to Brown and the other shop committee member that, as far as she was concerned, she had given Brown a clear and direct order to initial the work sheet on penalty of disciplinary action for refusal and that she had no choice but to suspend Brown for three days for refusing the order. "Shop stewards especially should understand insubordination," Sheldon said. "I can't have you setting this kind of example for the other workers."

Brown said that she would grieve the suspension.

Additional Relevant Information

ARTICLE V EMPLOYEE RESPONSIBILITIES

The employees shall comply with the Shop Regulations attached hereto and made part of this Agreement. It is understood that the Company has a right to make reasonable rules and that the Union has a right to grieve the application of such rules if it believes they are being unjustly applied.

ARTICLE X MANAGEMENT RIGHTS

The control of all matters concerning the operation and management of the plant and the operation of the Company's business are the exclusive responsibility of the Company, subject to the provisions of this Agreement.

The Company has the right to discharge, suspend, or otherwise discipline employees for cause.

SHOP REGULATION #9

The following are legitimate causes for disciplinary action that may result in suspension without pay or discharge: refusal to obey orders from a foreman or other supervisors; refusal to accept instructions or constructive criticism when given by a foreman or supervisor ....

Roles

UNION	MANAGEMENT
Grievant	Foreman
Shop Committee Chairman	General Supervisor

Role of the Grievant

Your name is Barry Faith. You have been employed as a loader/laborer by the Viking Machine Manufacturing Company since 1975. Viking is a fully integrated facility producing finished engine blocks from basic materials. Your responsibility is to prepare the finished block for shipment to purchasing companies.

On September 6 you were using a mechanical hoist to position engine blocks on a wooden pallet. There was much pressure on the shipping department that day because a number of orders had been completed at nearly the same time and all had to be shipped as soon as possible. The shipping area was becoming quite congested as towmotors delivered the blocks to be loaded on pallets which were then lifted by crane to the loading dock.

While you were working, your foreman, Harry Thiel, told you to start stacking engine blocks seven layers high on the pallets. You told him that it would put too much stress on the hoist to carry a load that high above the floor. He insisted that you stack the blocks as he told you, but you refused. You walked away, saying that you'd return in a moment with your steward.

Several minutes later you returned with Paul Marsh, your steward, who is also chairman of the union safety committee. Marsh told Thiel that he believed that it would be unsafe to load the blocks that high. Thiel told both of you that you had been given a direct, routine order and had refused to follow it. He said that you were already guilty of insubordination, but he'd give you another chance. Then he ordered you to load the blocks seven high. Marsh shook his head as if he couldn't believe the way the foreman was acting. You again refused.

Thiel told you to punch out immediately, because you were suspended for the rest of the day (half the shift). He said that a report of the incident would be put in your personnel file.

You and Marsh both told him that the union would grieve. He said, "Go ahead—but the rule is work now and grieve later."

Marsh said, "Not when safety is the issue." Thiel said that he didn't plan to discuss it any further and walked away. Marsh then told you that he'd write a report for Don Shearer, the shop committee chairman, and that you should talk to Shearer as soon as possible concerning the grievance.

Role of the Shop Committee Chairman

Your name is Donald Shearer. You are shop committee chairman for the union representing employees at the Viking Machine Manufacturing Company, which produces finished engine blocks from basic materials.

Shortly after lunch, you received the following report from Paul Marsh, zone steward for finishing and shipping. He is also chairman of the union safety committee.

> Don,
>
> At about 11 today, September 6, Barry Faith told me that Foreman Harry Thiel had ordered him to stack engine blocks seven layers high on pallets. Barry, a loader/laborer, told Thiel that it would put too much stress on the hoist to raise a block that high and refused to do the work. He told Thiel that he was going to get me.
>
> I returned with him to his work station several minutes later and told Thiel that I thought it was unsafe. Blocks are normally stacked five high on the pallets and occasionally six high. I think that seven high is unsafe, although we've never taken up this specific issue with the joint labor-management safety committee.
>
> Thiel was upset that Barry had refused his order. He said that he'd forget the insubordination already committed if Barry would do the work and ordered him again. Barry again refused. Thiel then suspended him for the rest of the shift, four hours, and said it would go on his record.
>
> To be honest, I think that Barry's main concern may have been trying to avoid getting too much work backed up for himself and his buddy on the next turn. It is really busy on the dock right now. He never actually mentioned safety when he first came to me, although he did say that he didn't think that the hoist could lift that high.
>
> I do think that it's a safety issue and that he legitimately refused the order on those grounds once I was there. I told him to fill you in on the details.

Role of the Foreman

Your name is Harry Thiel. You are foreman in Finishing/Shipping at the Viking Machine Manufacturing Company, where you've been employed for seven years. Viking manufactures finished engine blocks from basic parts.

Today, September 6, started an especially busy period in your department. Several orders had been completed at nearly the same time; they all must be shipped to customers as rapidly as possible. Beginning with yesterday's afternoon shift, the blocks began arriving at shipping as fast as they could be tagged and put aside. A considerable backlog is building up on the shipping floor and the loading dock and the towmotors are having trouble getting through.

At 11 this morning you told Barry Faith, a loader/laborer, to begin loading the engine blocks seven high on pallets. Faith refused to do the work, saying that his hoist should not be used to raise blocks that high off the floor. You again told him to do it, and he again refused, saying that it was not right. While you were in the midst of instructing him with a direct order, he walked away from you, saying that he'd return right away with his steward. You were steaming.

Faith returned several minutes later with Paul Marsh, the zone steward. Marsh said that the loading procedure was a safety hazard; he's also chairman of the union's safety committee. You calmly told Faith, in front of Marsh, that you'd forget the earlier insubordination if he'd do the work now as instructed. He refused again. You then suspended him for the remainder of the shift, four hours.

It was clear to you what was going on. It must have started on the midnight turn last night; it seems to happen every time things get busy and orders back up. The men get sensitive about a speedup; they have in mind a daily maximum quota even when things are busy. You know how things are; you were in the union.

Faith was trying to avoid having all that work stacked up around him and around his buddy on the next shift. The pressure of having pallets of engine blocks stacked seven high all around would be obvious—the loaders and shippers would have to work faster.

Faith didn't even mention safety until he returned with Marsh. Marsh raised the safety question. The only thing Faith ever said was that his hoist shouldn't be used to pile that high. It was the first excuse that he could think of to avoid doing the work.

As Marsh knows, the joint labor-management safety committee has never considered this issue. Blocks are normally stacked five high, but sometimes they're stacked six high even in nonpeak periods. It all depends on the pressure on shipping, the size of the order, the kind of trailer being loaded, etc. You were only trying to make more room on the shipping floor for the finished engine blocks that were backing up. You weren't trying to push Faith or anyone else to work faster.

There was no safety hazard. The order was a routine, legitimate directive to do a job in a specific manner. Faith was directly insubordinate, twice. The union is raising the safety issue only to cover the fact that discipline was appropriate. You'd better inform Charles Gilroy, the general supervisor, to expect a grievance.

Role of the General Supervisor

You are Charles Gilroy, general supervisor at the Viking Machine Manufacturing Company. Viking manufactures finished engine blocks from basic parts. You've worked for the firm for four years. It is your responsibility to coordinate all the operations and personnel aspects of the process at the level of the shop floor. All the foremen and their respective department superintendents report directly to you. You report to the manager of operations and have liaison responsibilities with the manager of employee relations. You are responsible for hearing and responding to union grievances, usually filed with you by Don Shearer, the union's shop committee chairman.

A little earlier this afternoon, the clerk gave you a phone message taken from Harry Thiel, the foreman in finishing/shipping. The note said that he had suspended Barry Faith, a loader/laborer, for the rest of his turn for insubordination. He refused to do a job in the manner specified by the foreman. According to the message, the union already has informed Thiel that it would file a grievance.

You'll want to get together with Thiel to find out what's behind the incident. He's one of your best foremen. You've given all foremen the latitude of suspending for the balance of the current shift without checking first with you if they're certain that the discipline is appropriate. They've all been given labor relations training in contract administration, and you have full faith in them.

Roles

UNION	MANAGEMENT
Grievant	Foreman
Grievance Committee	Employee Relations Director
Chairman	

Role of the Grievant

Your name is Ron Ford. You have been employed as an unskilled laborer by the Dutchman Cement Company since graduating from high school two years ago. Dutchman Cement is a large facility, producing cement for sale to area contractors as well as manufacturing many types of precast concrete forms and containers. As you drove to work today, November 6, you were excited because it seemed as if you were finally going to be able to sell your house. About a year ago, you and your wife bought a new house, but you've been unable to sell the old one because of the economy. It's been with five realtors already, the most recent one taking on the listing just two days ago. You hadn't even had a chance to deliver an extra key to the agent when he called last night to tell you that he was almost certain that he had a buyer.

The buyer was to come to town today to look at the house this morning. Since you're working the 7 to 3 shift this week, you arranged with the realtor to come to your present house this morning to pick up the key to the house that you're selling. You said that you'd leave it under the front door mat. It's an awkward arrangement, but your wife is away at her mother's and you can't afford to take any time off. A sale would be a tremendous relief. You've been laid off for three months and just got back to work two weeks ago. Even so, it is beginning to look like you will lose the new house if you can't sell the old one within the month. You can't make the payments anymore. The insecurity has also threatened your marriage.

About 9:30, you took a coffee break. When you reached into your pocket for change for the coffee machine, you discovered that you had brought the key with you, forgetting to leave it under the mat. The realtor said that he'd be at your house around 10; it's only about a 10-minute drive from the plant.

You went to find your foreman, Douglas Kuhlman, in an absolute panic to get permission to leave on an emergency. You couldn't locate him, so you placed the following note on his desk before leaving the plant.

Mr. Kuhlman—

I need permission to leave on an emergency. I forgot to leave the key to my old house for the real estate agent, and he has a buyer who needs to see the house this morning. I should be back within 25 to 30 minutes. Thank you.

Ron Ford

Just after you arrived at home, the realtor pulled up. You were able to give him the key and return immediately to the plant. You were gone a total of 30 minutes.

After getting back to your work station, you looked around for the foreman and saw him drinking coffee. You went over and asked, "Did you get my note ok?" He said that he didn't see any note.

"I had to leave for an emergency," you replied. "I was gone for half an hour so you'll have to dock my pay." Kuhlman responded that he wanted to read your note and then talk to you. You were relieved that he didn't seem angry.

About two hours later, the foreman returned and handed you a letter saying that you were being discharged for leaving the plant without permission. You told him that he was being unreasonable and didn't understand the circumstances. He wouldn't listen, so you told him that you were going to the union. You then saw your committeeman, John Fitz, who said that he'd fill in the grievance chairman, Al Gorden. Fitz told you to contact Gorden tomorrow to file the grievance.

Role of the Grievance Committee Chairman

Your name is Al Gorden, grievance committee chairman, Dutchman Cement Company. You received the following report from John Fitz, zone committeeman, this afternoon, November 6.

Al—

Ron Ford, a laborer in the cement casting department, was discharged by his foreman, Douglas Kuhlman, for leaving the plant without permission today.

Ford says that he left the plant because he had to return home to leave a key to his former house, which he hasn't been able to sell, for a realtor. Apparently the realtor had a prospective buyer and has just taken the listing, so Ford hadn't yet gotten a key to the old house to him.

After he got to work this morning, Ford realized that he had forgotten to leave the key. He couldn't find Kuhlman, so he left a note and then left the plant. He was gone 30 minutes.

Ford has been very depressed. He's been paying on both houses for a year and not long ago was on layoff for three months. It has gotten to the point where he'll lose his current house if he can't find a buyer because he just can't keep up both payments. It's also threatened his marriage to have so much instability and he's deeply in debt. He saw it as an emergency.

Obviously, he shouldn't have left without permission and I doubt that we can get him off completely, but at the very most he should be suspended. Besides, the company has not been consistent. In at least two other situations, men have left for emergencies without permission and were not disciplined. In one, a man had a gas leak at home and in the other his wife had just died.

Ford sincerely considered his situation to be a personal emergency. When he found the key in his pocket, he panicked. He has a good record—in two years, no discipline and only four days missed. We should be able to get the discharge reduced. Ford will tell you the details.

John

When grievances arise, you file them with George Zimmerman, employee relations director.

Role of the Foreman

Your name is Douglas Kuhlman. You are a foreman at the Dutchman Cement Company, where you've worked for 11 years, the last 5 as a foreman. Dutchman is a large facility, producing cement for sale to contractors as well as making many types of precast concrete forms and containers.

While you were drinking coffee today, November 6, Ron Ford, a laborer in the cement casting department, informed you that he had left the plant earlier on an emergency and that, since he could not find you, he left a note on your desk. You replied that you hadn't seen the note, but that you'd get it and talk to him later. He said that he had been gone half an hour and anticipated that you would dock his pay.

You went to the office and found his note:

Mr. Kuhlman—

I need permission to leave on an emergency. I forgot to leave the key to my old house for the real estate agent, and he has a buyer who needs to see the house this morning. I should be back within 25 to 30 minutes. Thank you.

Ron Ford

You were upset that Ford had taken it upon himself to leave without permission; when you read the note, you were very angry. You could barely believe that Ford had been so foolish as to consider such a reason an actual emergency.

Ford has been a good employee. He has no disciplinary record and has missed only four days of work with the company. But he is an unskilled laborer; plenty of high school graduates would like to have his job. A business won't compete long if its employees have the kind of attitude that Ford displayed toward the company and his job.

You talked the situation over with George Zimmerman, employee relations director. Zimmerman is really a hard-liner about employee conduct. He told you that he thought there was no reason to keep someone who would be so outrageous as to just pick up and leave the plant. In his opinion, Ford should be discharged. You agreed and he told you to write him the notice effective immediately.

You gave Ford the notice this afternoon. He was upset and said that he was going to the union. You'd better notify Zimmerman to expect a grievance.

Role of the Employee Relations Director

Your name is George Zimmerman. You've been employed as employee relations director at the Dutchman Cement Company for the past 12 years. Dutchman is a large facility, producing cement for sale to contractors as well as making many types of precast concrete forms and containers. You run a tight ship and are not unhappy about your reputation as a hard-liner when it comes to employee discipline. Because the company employs a large number of unskilled laborers for heavy work, there is always a ready supply of employees to take the place of anyone who won't work or who displays a poor attitude.

Earlier today, November 6, one of the foremen, Doug Kuhlman, reported to you that a laborer in the cement casting department had left the plant without permission. Kuhlman was upset, not only because the worker, Ron Ford, had left but also because of his reason. Ford had forgotten to leave a key under the mat at home so that a real estate agent could show the house to a prospective buyer.

Kuhlman explained that Ford had been a good employee; he had no disciplinary record and had missed only four days of work in his two years with the company. But, he argued, leaving the plant for such a reason was outrageous and was especially serious because he hadn't gotten permission. Ford was gone half an hour.

He suggested that Ford be discharged and you agreed. There was no need to keep an employee who would act so foolishly. You told Kuhlman to write the notice to Ford, discharging him immediately. As far as you can remember, there were only two instances in the past where workers left for emergencies. They weren't disciplined in either case, but then they left for real emergencies. One man's wife had just died and the other learned of a gas leak at his house. Ford's case is certainly not an emergency.

No doubt there will be a grievance soon enough from Al Gorden, the union's grievance committee chairman.

Roles

UNION	MANAGEMENT
Grievant	Supervisor
Shop Steward	General Manager

Role of the Grievant

Your name is Eugene Bischof. You have been employed by Evergreen Auto Sales, Inc., as a paint and body technician for three years. Friday, April 18, you finished your lunch about 10 minutes before the end of your break and walked to a vending machine in the lunch room to get a bag of potato chips.

The machine, which seems constantly to be malfunctioning, has a large glass panel about 2 feet by 3 feet across the bottom, allowing the customer to see the bag of chips fall into a bin at the bottom of the machine. You put in your money, but the package fell only partway from its slot, sticking between the slot and the glass. This happens so often that the owner and servicer of the machines, VENDCO, has arranged for employees to get refunds directly from the Evergreen bookkeeper.

You thought that you could easily dislodge the bag, so you tapped against the glass with the heel of your hand. The bag did not drop, so you rocked the machine while still tapping the glass. Suddenly the glass shattered and your hand went through the broken glass into the bin. You received scratches on your forearm but no serious injury. Retrieving the chips, you walked immediately to the office of your supervisor, Louis DeLuca, to explain what happened. You offered to pay for the damage and apologized. DeLuca said that he'd look at the machine and take care of it and told you to put some antiseptic ointment on your arm and go back to work.

Upon finishing work for the day, you walked through the lunch room on your way to the time clock and noticed that the glass had been repaired already. DeLuca came out of his office and asked to speak with you. Once inside, he handed you a letter informing you that you were suspended for three days for damaging company property. He explained that he believed you deliberately vandalized the machine and that repair of the glass had cost the company $48 in materials and labor. You begin to protest, saying that it was an accident and you had offered to pay. He cut you off and told you that the decision was final.

Very angry, you tried to find the shop steward, Bill Devlin, but he had already left for home. Besides being unfair, this was the first discipline of any kind on your record. (The only incidents in the past were only some warnings for outbursts of your temper, which is a little hot.) On the way home, you ran over the entire incident in your mind and remembered that

Pete Smelko from the shop and a woman from bookkeeping were also in the lunch room and might serve as witnesses. Upon arriving home, you called Bill Devlin and arranged to meet with him tomorrow morning, Saturday, to talk about filing a grievance the first thing on Monday, when your suspension begins.

Role of the Supervisor

Your name is Louis DeLuca. You are a supervisor at Evergreen Auto Sales, Inc. You've worked for Evergreen for 15 years, starting in the shop, and have been a supervisor for 4 years. You direct the mechanics, paint and body technicians, and maintenance personnel.

Around noon on Friday, April 18, Eugene Bischof, a paint and body technician with three years' service, came into your office. He explained that he had accidentally broken the glass on a vending machine in the lunch room. He offered to pay for the damage, but you told him that you wanted to look at the machine and discuss it with him later. You also saw to it that he put some antiseptic on his scratched arm before he returned to work.

When you walked into the lunch room, you found broken glass scattered over the floor as far as six feet from the machine. What was broken was the large 2-foot by three-foot panel at the bottom, through which the customer sees the choice drop into a bin. The machine had a large dent in its side, obviously from kicking, and was pushed from its normal position. You were convinced that the amount of damage couldn't have occurred from a simple accident. Two other employees were just leaving the room: Pete Smelko from the shop and a woman from bookkeeping, whom you didn't know by name. You asked what had happened. They just said that Bischof had hit the machine to try to get something out and broke the glass. You told them both to report to the general manager's office to give statements of what they saw, which could be notarized by the cashier.

You are convinced that Bischof purposely damaged the machine and are angered that he tried to mislead you. He has quite a temper; although he has not been a serious disciplinary problem, he has been warned several times about mouthing off when given an order.

The vending machines, owned and serviced by VENDCO, Inc., have been a problem. Recently, to prevent vandalism, the company arranged with VENDCO that any employee who lost money could get an immediate refund from bookkeeping; VENDCO would then reimburse Evergreen. This policy was announced to the union, to all employees in the company newsletter, and on posters in the lunch room and on all vending machines.

Proceeds from the vending machines go to a general slush fund used at the discretion of the general manager. It is usually used for expenses such as seed money for the company picnic, small gifts for employees at Christmas and retirement, and advances on travel expenses for managers and supervisors.

You called VENDCO, explaining the problem, and it contacted a glass company, which completed the replacement work by 3. The bill to Evergreen, which is responsible for all expenses due to vandalism and damage under the agreement with VENDCO, was $48. There was no way to repair the dent and VENDCO said that it doesn't make such repairs unless a machine is completely out of commission.

The machines were damaged with some frequency before the new policy, but no one was ever caught before. Since the new policy, things have improved greatly. You decided that Bischof had to be disciplined and gave him a three-day suspension letter at the end of his shift after explaining your rationale. You'll want to report it to Rose Halliwell, the general manager.

Role of the Shop Steward

Your name is Bill Devlin. You are parts supervisor for Evergreen Auto Sales, Inc., and shop steward for employees of the mechanical, auto body, and maintenance departments. You've worked for Evergreen for 10 years, and have been shop steward for the last five years.

One of the paint and body technicians, Gene Bischof, called you just after you arrived home from work tonight, Friday, April 18, about 4:30. He's been in the shop for about three years. While a bit of a hothead, he is a decent worker and union member.

Bischof was very excited on the phone, saying that he'd been suspended for accidentally damaging some vending machine. You couldn't get the details clearly from him because he was so angry. You've arranged to meet him the next morning to talk over the situation and decide how to write up a grievance.

As best you could decipher from the phone call, Bischof must have broken the glass on a vending machine that had taken his money. The machines have been quite a problem, and a good bit of damage has occurred. They're dented and scratched; in general, the worse they look and the more they malfunction, the worse they're mistreated.

The company recently announced to the union that it had worked out an arrangement with VENDCO, the owner and servicer of the machines, to have refunds for lost money given on the spot by the Evergreen bookkeeping department. VENDCO then apparently reimburses Evergreen. That seems to have helped the damage problem somewhat. The commission from the machines, which are located in the lunch room and used heavily, is probably substantial. You have no idea what Evergreen does with the money—it's probably someone's private slush fund.

In pursuing the grievance, you'll have to deal with Rose Halliwell, the general manager, and Lou DeLuca, Bischof's supervisor. From the little information that you were able to get from Bischof, this seems like a decent grievance. No one should be disciplined for accidentally damaging a machine.

Role of the General Manager

117

Case 6:
Through
the Looking
Glass

Your name is Rose Halliwell. You are general manager of Evergreen Auto Sales, Inc. You've been with the company in various capacities for 18 years.

This afternoon you got a call from Lou DeLuca, supervisor of the mechanical, body, and maintenance departments, about damage to one of the vending machines by a shop employee. DeLuca said that he was convinced that it was deliberate and he wanted to suspend the employee. You agreed but told him that you wanted a full report on the details.

The vending machines have been a frustrating part of your job. They're owned and serviced by VENDCO; Evergreen gets a substantial commission from them since they're located in the lunch room and used heavily. But they're constantly malfunctioning, leading to increasing employee abuse of the machines.

Besides the morale problem that the situation causes, you were especially concerned because the proceeds go to a slush fund under your control, used for seed money for events like the company picnic and also as advance money for managers and supervisors to cover traveling expenses for company business. You recently worked out an agreement with VENDCO that Evergreen's bookkeeping department would make direct refunds to employees who lost money in the machines and VENDCO would reimburse Evergreen. Evergreen takes responsibility for the repair costs for any damage to the machines in view of the high commission that VENDCO pays.

You had been hoping that the new policy would alleviate the problem. It was communicated to the union and to all employees through signs on the machines and in the company newsletter. No doubt the union will grieve.

STATEMENT OF JANET PAGE

On Friday, April 18, I was in the lunch room shortly before noon when one of the shop employees, whose name I do not know, began to pound with his hand on one of the vending machines that took his money. He hit the glass panel at the bottom, then rocked the machine back and forth a little. The glass broke, and he hurt his arm.

I wasn't watching closely enough to know whether he deliberately damaged the machine. Since I work in bookkeeping myself, I certainly would have just gone there and gotten a refund. But the machines are always malfunctioning, they're all scratched and dented, and he isn't the only employee I've seen pounding or even kicking them.

Janet Page, Bookkeeping

STATEMENT OF PETER SMELKO

I was leaving the lunch room around noon on Friday, April 18, when I heard a racket behind me in the vending area. I turned around to see

Gene Bischof, a paint and body technician, rocking a vending machine back and forth and then, pressing on the glass panel at the bottom, breaking the glass.

I don't think that he deliberately tried to damage the machine but he did work it over a bit. It's no wonder—all the machines are scratched and dented and never repaired. They rarely work. Personally I've gotten so tired of losing money in them that I don't use them anymore.

Bischof just did what anyone does when one of those machines rips off your money. It wasn't his fault that the glass broke.

Peter Smelko, Shop Mechanic

Other Relevant Information

ARTICLE III MANAGEMENT RIGHTS

Management reserves all rights relating to the direction of the work force, scheduling, production decisions, the use of facilities, and all other functions necessary to the efficient and profitable conduct of the business except as specifically limited in this agreement. Management has the right to promulgate specific work rules in its direction of the work force which shall be binding on all employees.

ARTICLE VII DISCIPLINE AND DISCHARGE

Employees will be discharged, suspended, or otherwise disciplined only for proper cause. Except where circumstances require a more serious or prompt management action, progressive discipline will be utilized.

ARTICLE VIII GRIEVANCE PROCEDURE

Disputes arising under this agreement will first be discussed informally between the employee, or the employee and the steward, or the steward alone, and the employee's supervisor. If not satisfactorily resolved, the grievance must be reduced to writing within 10 days of the date of the incident or situation giving rise to the grievance. The supervisor must provide a written response within 5 days of receipt of the written grievance. If not satisfactorily resolved at that step, the grievance may be appealed to the General Manager within 5 days of the receipt of the supervisor's response. The General Manager shall have 10 days in which to respond. If not satisfactorily resolved, the union may demand arbitration within 30 days of the receipt of the General Manager's response.

WORK RULE #19 VANDALISM

Employees may not mark, deface, or otherwise willfully damage, neglect, or sabotage company property or equipment. Vandalism shall be treated as a major offense.

Roles

UNION	MANAGEMENT
Grievant	Foreman
Chief Shop Steward	Labor Relations Officer

Role of the Grievant

Your name is Lou Costo. You have been employed by the Red River Meat Company since 1965. At the end of the shift on January 20, you were sitting in the locker room, changing, when you noticed that someone had written on the back of the locker room door "Costo's wife is a pig." Very angry, you were able to wash and rub away most of the writing.

You then went looking for Al Meyer, certain that he had done it. You and Meyer have never gotten along and had words just last week on the job. He has been harassing you all this week and has made several abusive comments about your wife, who works as a waitress at a restaurant that he frequents.

Seeing him about to leave the plant, you confronted Meyer and accused him of writing the graffiti. He denied doing it. You called him a "God-damn liar" and he called you a "fat son-of-a-bitch."

While you were exchanging words, Clifford Clark, the foreman, demanded that both of you step in to his office. Clark told both of you to cool off and asked what the argument was about. Grabbing Meyer's arm, you said, "This son-of-a-bitch wrote 'Costo's wife is a pig' on the back of the locker room door."

"She might be," Meyer responded, "but I didn't write it." He then pushed you away, saying "Get your fat hands off of me." You called him a "son-of-a-bitch" again and shoved him out of the supervisor's office. Meyer was coming back in to throw a punch when Clark stepped between you and ordered Meyer to leave the plant immediately. Clark then told you that using abusive language toward another employee and fighting on company property are against plant rules. He reminded you that you had received a written warning for abusive language just last fall, ordered you to leave immediately, and said that you were suspended for the next working day.

You left, assuring him that you'd be filing a grievance with your steward, Roy Shelly. You phoned Shelly as soon as you got home. He said that he'd report the matter to Richard Hiner, the chief steward, and that you should see Hiner as soon as you got back to work to file a grievance.

Role of the Chief Shop Steward

Your name is Richard Hiner. You are chief shop steward at the Red River Meat Company, where you've worked for nine years. You just received the following report from Roy Shelly, zone committeeman.

> Lou Costo is on a one-day suspension today for an incident that occurred yesterday, January 20. The incident took place in Foreman Clifford Clark's office. Costo supposedly swore at and pushed Al Meyer, another employee in the same department.
>
> Costo told me that Meyer had written "Costo's wife is a pig" on the back of the locker room door. Costo was confronting Meyer when both were called into Clark's office.
>
> Meyer says that he didn't write the graffiti. I don't think that we ever will know if he did or didn't, although from his attitude, I'd guess that he did. Anyway, it can't be proved.
>
> The point is that Costo was very shaken when he read the graffiti. He failed to settle it with Meyer and when they exchanged words in the Foreman's office, Costo grabbed Meyer's arm and swore at him. Meyer pushed Costo back and Costo then shoved Meyer out through the open office door.
>
> Clark immediately suspended Costo for one day without trying to get to the bottom of the situation even though he had both of them in his office. Costo already has a written reprimand for abusive language, which apparently is a special bug with Clark.
>
> We should be able to turn the company around on this one. The shift had ended and the two were trying to settle their differences when Clark intervened. Swearing is common around the plant and, in view of these circumstances, probably healthy. The pushing and shoving were just minor fisticuffs.
>
> Both men were upset and angry. Costo shouldn't get suspended.
>
> I told Costo to talk with you and that you'd file the grievance with Mrs. Watson in labor relations.

Role of the Foreman

Your name is Clifford Clark. You have been a foreman at the Red River Meat Company for six years. Before your promotion to foreman, you were a union member, employed as a machine operator.

On January 20, at the end of the shift, you were standing near the plant gate when you noticed a loud discussion between Lou Costo and Al Meyer. You knew that they didn't get along well and that Costo had a very bad temper. In fact, you had given him a written warning November 2 for using abusive language toward a shipping clerk at whom he swore repeatedly. You heard swearing and, afraid there might be a fight, called Costo and Meyer to your office.

You asked what the beef was about. Costo said that Meyer had written abusive graffiti about Mrs. Costo on the locker room door. Meyer denied everything but, when he said "maybe she is, but I didn't write it," the two started at each other again. Costo called Meyer a "son-of-a-bitch" and pushed him through the open office doorway.

You ordered Meyer to leave immediately. You then told Costo that swearing, abusive language, and fighting could not be tolerated. Reminding him that he had been warned previously for abusive language, you told him to clean up and go home and that he was suspended the next day.

Costo left, saying that he would file a grievance.

Role of the Labor Relations Officer

Your name is Betty Watson. You have been labor relations officer at the Red River Meat Company for the past year and a half. Your responsibilities include handling all union grievances filed against the company.

In your morning mail today, January 21, you received the following memo from Foreman Clifford Clark.

January 20

Subject: Disciplinary Action Report
To: Mrs. Betty Watson
From: Clifford Clark

At the close of the shift today, I suspended Lou Costo for one day for abusive language toward another employee and fighting.

After the shift had ended, I saw Costo and Al Meyer, another employee, having an argument. I called them into my office to try to settle the dispute. Costo was very angry, accusing Meyer of writing abusive graffiti about Costo's wife on the locker room wall.

Before I could calm them down, the two exchanged curses as Costo grabbed Meyer by the arm. Meyer pushed him off, saying that maybe his wife was a pig (what had been written on the wall) but that he didn't write it. Costo then called him a "son-of-a-bitch" and shoved him out of my office.

Costo has a very bad temper and I had given him a written warning last November 2 for very abusive language toward a shipping clerk. He swore at her repeatedly. I told him to leave immediately and that he was suspended for one day, tomorrow.

Since everything occurred in my office, there was no need to investigate further. We can't tolerate abusive language and fighting. Costo has been warned before. I think that the one-day suspension is valid progressive discipline but would recommend that it be no heavier since both men were involved.

Roles

UNION	MANAGEMENT
Grievant	Foreman
Chief Steward	Plant Superintendent

Role of the Grievant

Your name is Carl Woodruff. You have been employed as a parts inspector for the past six years at the Harmonic Speaker Company. Harmonic makes speakers for automobile radio systems. Your job requires that you constantly inspect soldered speaker parts that pass before you on a conveyer belt and that the parts are centered on the belt. After passing your station, the parts enter a long, heated chamber that ensures that they are totally dry before final assembly, which occurs further down the line. The size and shape of the speakers have changed since the heating chamber was installed, so there is now little clearance for the parts that you inspect. If a part doesn't clear the chamber entrance, it falls from the conveyer belt and must be reassembled. You work alone and cannot speak easily to anyone else in your section because of the required attention to your job. Other inspectors in your section do similar work at different stages in the process; like you, they can see other workers but cannot communicate easily with them.

This morning, January 5, you were at your station checking the parts as they passed. Everything was going fine except that you had a severe case of indigestion, and, as usual in your job, you were very bored. Without any warning, the section foreman, William Burgan, started yelling at you, complaining that you were goofing off. You said that he was crazy; you were just doing your job.

You asked what the problem was. He said that you were deliberately burping loudly to get the attention of the other workers. You denied it. He said that it was obvious that you were engaging in horseplay and that it was disrupting other workers. He told you that horseplay was against the rules and pointed out that your own inattention to what you were supposed to be doing could result in lost production. He said that he would be writing you up.

An hour later, Burgan returned and gave you a letter stating that you were suspended for the next two days for horseplay. You couldn't believe it. Your only other disciplinary incident was about eight months ago, when Burgan warned you about horseplay. That time you actually were caught. You and several others had been kicking rejected parts back and forth to each other on the floor as the line went by. You thought that Burgan might be out for you, and this proves it. You told him that it's just a difference of opinion, his word against yours.

You told Burgan that you'd be seeing the chief steward, Fred Cardellino, to file a grievance.

Role of the Chief Steward

Your name is Fred Cardellino. You are chief steward of the union representing employees of the Harmonic Speaker Company, which makes speakers for automobile radios. Earlier today, January 5, Carl Woodruff told you that he had been suspended for two days and wanted to file a grievance.

Woodruff is a parts inspector whose job is to inspect components passing before him on a conveyer belt before they enter a long drying chamber. He said that everything on the line was running smoothly this morning when his foreman, William Burgan, started yelling and complaining that he was goofing off by burping loudly to catch the attention of the other employees and distract them from their work.

Woodruff denied the charge. The foreman said that it was obvious that he was burping loudly and continuously, engaging in horseplay in violation of the rules. Woodruff said that he did have a bad case of indigestion but that he wasn't doing anything. Besides, he said, horseplay has to involve others and this is just a difference of opinion—Burgan's word against his. Woodruff said that the other workers would testify that they didn't notice him doing anything.

When you asked why the foreman would make such a charge, Woodruff said that Burgan might be out for him since he had given Woodruff a written warning for horseplay eight months ago. The earlier incident involved several workers kicking rejected parts back and forth between them on the floor as the line went by—the kind of thing that often goes on to break the monotony of that sort of job.

You file grievances with Robert Terek, the plant superintendent.

Role of the Foreman

You are William H. Burgan, a foreman at the Harmonic Speaker Company, which makes speakers for automobile radios. This morning, January 5, you were with Emil Francheski, the quality control superintendent, near the east gate of the plant when you heard a parts inspector, Carl Woodruff, burping loudly and continuously. It became quickly obvious to you that he was doing it deliberately to get the attention of other workers. Woodruff's job is to inspect components passing before him on a conveyer belt before they enter a long drying chamber. He also has to be sure that the parts are centered on the belt, because there is little clearance at the entrance to the chamber. Parts that don't clear the entrance fall to the floor and must be completely reassembled. Because the size and shape of the speakers have changed since the drying chamber was installed, nearly every part could fall if the inspector weren't alert.

You moved to observe more closely and were even more convinced that Woodruff was doing the burping act deliberately, to get the attention of others. It's the kind of thing that goes on all the time to kill the boredom of the jobs, but you've got to stop it because it inevitably results in lost production. You walked across the floor to confront him. As soon as you got near, he stopped. You asked why he was pulling such a stunt for the others and reminded him that he could have been responsible for lost production. He denied everything.

You're tired of juvenile activities. Just eight months ago, you warned Woodruff for horseplay. That time he and others were kicking rejected parts back and forth to each other on the floor as the line went by. You told him that you'd be back to write him up. He said that it was just a difference of opinion, your word against his. That made you even more angry.

You checked his file to confirm the earlier warning, then contacted Robert Terek, the plant superintendent, and recommended a two-day suspension. He agreed and authorized you to notify Woodruff. You did; Woodruff told you that he would be seeing Fred Cardellino, the chief steward, to file a grievance.

Role of the Plant Superintendent

Your name is Robert Terek. You are plant superintendent at the Harmonic Speaker Company, which manufactures speaker systems for automobile radios. You've had your position for the past five years. Earlier today, January 5, Foreman Bill Burgan consulted you about a disciplinary problem.

Burgan said that he'd caught Carl Woodruff, a parts inspector, burping loudly and continuously to get the attention of other workers on the conveyer line where he works. Burgan said that Woodruff's burping could lead to his own and others' inattention, causing lost production.

Burgan said that Woodruff denied everything. He had given Woodruff an official warning eight months ago for another incident of horseplay and said that he was tired of this kind of juvenile activity. You wish that you didn't have to get involved with this level of decision but recognize that the foremen are expected to keep discipline and must be supported. Burgan does a reasonably good job, although he is quite strict. He recommended a two-day suspension in view of the earlier offense. You questioned him closely to be certain that he was sure of his observations and to confirm the details of the earlier incident of horseplay. Then you agreed and told Burgan to give Woodruff the notice. He told you that he was with Emil Francheski, who might be a witness.

No doubt you'll get a grievance from Fred Cardellino, the union's chief steward. You're quite certain that none of the workers will be a witness against a union brother, so there's no point in asking others if they heard Woodruff. You told your secretary to tell Francheski to go to plant security to give a written statement.

ARTICLE XII

The Company will not discipline or discharge employees except for cause. Progressive discipline will be used except that in the case of major offenses, the penalty may include suspension or discharge.

PLANT RULE 7

Theft, fighting, gambling and horseplay occurring on company property are strictly prohibited and are considered to be among the major offenses that may lead to suspension or discharge.

STATEMENT OF EMIL FRANCHESKI

My name is Emil Francheski. I am the superintendent of quality control for the Harmonic Speaker Company.

On the morning of January 5, I was with William H. Burgan, foreman. Foreman Burgan noticed some irregularities in the vicinity of the drying chamber and went closer for observation. He said to me, "Look at Woodruff, the parts inspector, goofing off."

We were approximately 30 feet away. Burgan said, "Listen to what he's doing." I heard what sounded like two burps, about a minute apart. I couldn't tell for sure that it was Woodruff, and I don't know how many other employees may have heard the burps.

As Burgan was confronting Woodruff, I went on to my desk in the QC office.

s/Emil Francheski
taken by G. Johnson
Plant Security
5 January

CASE 9: BARRED FOR FIGHTING

Roles

UNION	MANAGEMENT
Grievant	General Manager
Business Agent	Regional Personnel Representative

Role of the Grievant

Your name is Dan Bennett. You have been employed by the Bluefield Supermarket, a unit of the Quality Market Group, for eight years. You began as a stock clerk and now manage the produce department. James Emmel, the general manager and supervisor of all employees, has been complaining all summer that you should help unload the warehouse trucks. You frequently do help with produce and you sometimes help unload when trucks are backed up at the dock, but you believe that unloading is clearly a stock clerk job and not yours—and you should know since you've done both. You have enough other work to do that you're not interested in having to unload every truck that arrives.

On September 12 you were at the Canopy Tavern. You were sitting at the bar, having a drink, when Jim Emmel and an attractive woman walked past you and took stools at the other end. A few minutes later you walked over to them and offered to buy them a round of drinks. Emmel introduced you to Kathleen Phillips, the new regional personnel representative for all the stores in the Quality Market Group. She said that they appreciated your offer but had already ordered.

Emmel then said to Phillips, "Dan is produce manager at Bluefield and a good worker except that he doesn't unload trucks." You replied, "Why don't you just get off my ass about unloading trucks, Emmel. You know that it's not my job." Angered by your response, Emmel said, "Why don't you just move your lazy bones and go back and finish your drink."

At that, you blew up, and took a shot at Emmel's face. He saw it coming and started moving away, taking only a hard slap. Seeing that the incident was causing a commotion, you then just said, "Nice meeting you, Ms. Phillips," turned, and walked back to your stool. Phillips told the bartender that she wanted to see the manager and walked into the restaurant area. Within a few minutes, the manager came over to you and told you to finish your drink and leave.

When you arrived at work the following morning, a note in your time card slot told you to report to the service desk. There the clerk gave you an envelope that contained a letter stating that you were discharged for fighting, effective immediately.

You contacted your steward, Mel Minzer, and gave him a full report. He said that he'd fill in Arthur Noon, the union's business agent, who would file a grievance on your behalf within a day. He also told you to be sure to tell Noon everything when he contacts you.

Role of the Business Agent

Your name is Arthur Noon. You are business agent for the union representing the employees of the Bluefield Supermarket as well as other employees who work for supermarkets in the Quality Market Group. You just received the following report from Melvin Minzer, steward at Bluefield.

> Art:
>
> On September 12, Dan Bennett saw Jim Emmel, general manager at Bluefield, and Kathleen Phillips, regional personnel representative for Quality Market Group, in the Canopy Tavern. Dan had been drinking and went over and offered to buy drinks for Emmel and Phillips, whom he did not know.
>
> Dan says that Emmel introduced Phillips, then made a derogatory comment about Dan's work. Dan took it as a cheap shot in front of the new personnel rep. Apparently they've had a running disagreement over whether Dan is obligated to help unload trucks. He works as produce manager. He was a stock clerk. There are no job descriptions.
>
> Dan had words with Emmel and admits that he slapped him in the face. Dan says that he tried to slug him but Emmel backed away, so it was only a slap. Phillips reported the incident to the manager and had Dan thrown out of the tavern.
>
> When Dan went to work the next morning, he received a discharge letter for fighting.
>
> In the first place, I think that the incident has been exaggerated. Dan has a good record and is a hard worker. He doesn't deserve a discharge. More importantly, what happened is between Dan and Emmel and is not a company affair.
>
> I don't think that the company had just cause. The management rights clause applies only to events within the supermarket and only in an employer-employee context.
>
> I told Dan to be prepared to fill you in so that you can file a grievance right away.
>
> Mel

Role of the General Manager

Your name is James Emmel. You are general manager of the Bluefield Supermarket, a unit of the Quality Market Group. Included in your responsibilities is the direction of all employees. Over the summer months, you've repeatedly had run-ins with Dan Bennett, the produce manager. You've told him (and everyone else, for that matter) that you expect them to help out when asked to assist in unloading trucks from the warehouse. He has helped on occasion but maintains that it's not his job and hasn't been since he left the position of stock clerk several years ago. It is a primary part of the stock clerk's job to unload the trucks, but you expect all employees to be available to assist when needed. There are no formal job descriptions.

On September 12 you and Kathleen Phillips, the new regional personnel representative for the Quality Market Group, went to the Canopy Tavern to discuss business over drinks and dinner. After you had ordered drinks at the bar, Dan Bennett came over and offered to buy you a round of drinks. Since you had already ordered, Phillips declined and you introduced them. You told her about Dan's job as produce manager and made light of the dispute that you've had about unloading. Apparently he didn't like your tone of voice because he told you to "get off his ass." When you told him to go back to his drink, he reached behind Phillips and hit you in the face. He tried to take a full punch, but you backed away, getting only a hard slap. You were mad enough to go after him, but Phillips calmed you down. She then reported the incident to the manager, who threw Bennett out of the tavern. You knew that Bennett was in deep trouble so you felt less insulted.

Over dinner in the restaurant, you and Phillips discussed the incident. She believed that Bennett should be discharged immediately, noting that because of the conversation and the entire circumstances, the incident was clearly work-related and not just a private matter. In her view, the company should not tolerate employees striking supervisors. You agreed, and Bennett was notified by letter when he reported for work the next morning that he was discharged.

No doubt the union will grieve the discharge. But since Phillips is responsible for handling grievances once they leave an individual market and consults with market general managers even at the early steps, you feel quite secure.

Role of the Regional Personnel Representative

Your name is Kathleen Phillips. You have recently begun working for the Quality Market Group as regional personnel representative. Your responsibilities include personnel relations for a regional division of the group, including 12 stores. You work in a liaison capacity with the general manager of each store and handle all grievances and arbitrations once they leave the earliest step in the grievance process.

On September 12 you visited the Bluefield Supermarket to meet General Manager Jim Emmel. He suggested continuing the business discussion over drinks and dinner, and you agreed. You arrived at the Canopy Tavern and took seats at the end of the bar for drinks. Shortly after you ordered, a man who was later introduced by Emmel as Dan Bennett, produce manager at his supermarket, came over and offered to buy you drinks. You declined since you had just ordered.

Emmel said that Bennett was a good employee "except that he didn't like to unload trucks." He said it in a joking way, and you assumed it was an inside joke. Bennett reacted angrily, telling Emmel to "get off his ass about the trucks." Emmel told him to go back to his drink, but Bennett took a swing at Emmel around your back, slapping him hard in the face. You reported the incident to the manager, who ejected Bennett.

Over dinner, you told Emmel that you thought Bennett should be discharged. Although the incident did not occur at work, it was clearly work-related since the entire context of the conversation and altercation was the employer-employee relationship. Emmel explained to you that he's had a hard time getting Bennett to help unload warehouse trucks because Bennett claims that it's not part of his job as produce manager. Apparently he was a stock clerk previously and no longer wants to do any part of that job except when he sees fit. There are no formal job descriptions.

Emmel agreed that Bennett should be discharged and said that he'd notify Bennett the next day. No doubt you'll be hearing from the union with a grievance. You've been told that the business agent is Arthur Noon.

Additional Relevant Information

ARTICLE III MANAGEMENT RIGHTS
The Union recognizes that the management of the company and the direction of the working forces is vested exclusively in the employer, and this shall include, but not be limited to, the right to discharge, suspend, or discipline for cause, as well as to promulgate reasonable rules and regulations.

WORK RULE 14 DISCHARGE WITHOUT NOTICE
Although progressive discipline will be followed for all nonmajor offenses, major offenses may carry with them the penalty of immediate discharge without advanced notice. Major offenses under this rule include carrying concealed weapons; fighting or attempting to cause bodily injury to another; gambling; drunkenness; conduct that violates the standards of common decency or morality in the community.

Roles

UNION	MANAGEMENT
Two Grievants	Employee Relations Manager
Union President	Personnel Assistant for
	Equal Employment
	Opportunity and
	Affirmative Action

Roles of the Grievants

Your names are Nick Matus and Andy Bernat, good friends who have been employed by Quantum Electric Supply Company since 1976. You work in a three-person productivity group in the lighting department with Virginia Piper, who was hired about three weeks ago. The three of you get along fine, although things were even better when Charlie Freid, the former member of your group who was replaced by Virginia, was working with you. He left for a job in Houston. Virginia is one of the few women in your department. Most of the women working in the production departments have been hired in just the last two or three years.

It has been a common practice among the workers in your department to ambush a coworker who has become engaged. On the way to the locker room at the end of the shift, he is stripped and thrown in the shower. When it became known last week that Virginia had just become engaged, the guys began daring each other to give her the standard congratulations party. The few women who work in the shop have their own small locker room but no shower. Since "arranging the party" would be easiest for you two, because you work closely with her, you accepted the dare.

The task of your productivity group is to assemble light fixtures. Someone in the group must leave periodically to get more components from the supply room. At the end of the shift, it's customary to restock the work station completely for the incoming crew on the next shift. As agreed among the men, toward the end of the shift yesterday, June 11, the two of you told Virginia that you were going to the supply room to restock components. The supply room is right beside the men's locker room. The plan was to wait until just before the end of the shift to call Virginia to the supply room where you two would quickly do the stripping and then carry her into the locker room and the shower, where all the other partygoers would be waiting to convey their congratulations.

You called to Virginia and asked her to come to the supply room to help with the last box of components. When she came in, you quickly closed the door. Nick grabbed her around the waist from behind, telling her not to worry and explaining that this was the traditional engagement congratulations. Andy tried to unbutton her shirt, telling her that all you would be doing is throwing her in the shower. (There had been some dares to strip her completely, but everyone assumed that she'd probably end up going into the shower with most of her clothes on, either because you two would chicken out or because she'd put up a fight.) Virginia did put up a fight and started screaming. You let her go and she ran from the room, accompanied by the boos of some of the guys waiting outside, some yelling that she should come back, that it was "all in good fun."

Virginia apparently went directly to the department supervisor, J.W. Rhoades, who appeared at the locker room just as you were leaving for home. He told you that he wanted to see you in his office immediately. You went, but not before finding your shop steward, Lenny Colosimo, to go along. A number of the guys also went with you for moral support.

In the office, Rhoades confronted you with the story that he had heard from Virginia Piper. You didn't deny being in the supply room or trying to take off her shirt. But you both strongly denied attempting to harm or molest her in any way, explaining that it was part of the standard party since she had just become engaged. The men who had accompanied you agreed, telling Rhoades that it was all in good fun. Rhoades knew about the standard party; the supervisors generally looked the other way when it happened unless things got so rowdy that someone might be hurt. When you told him that's what was going on, he blew up, saying that he couldn't believe that you would be so stupid and irresponsible.

Rhoades said that what you had done was so serious that he was suspending both of you immediately, pending a full investigation into the incident. He also said that you might be fired for your actions and that, if he were you, he'd give some thought to getting a lawyer in case Virginia decided to press charges. Colosimo, your steward, tried to talk Rhoades out of the suspension, but Rhoades only got more angry. Colosimo then told Rhoades that the union would be grieving his discipline. When you all left the office, Colosimo told both of you to make arrangements to see Martin Lowes, the union president, to tell him the complete details and said that he'd send a report to Lowes to fill him in beforehand.

Role of the Union President

Your name is Martin Lowes. You are president of the union local that represents employees of the Quantum Electric Supply Company. You work on the evening shift and found the following note from the shop steward, Leonard Colosimo, when you came in for the 11 p.m. shift today, June 11:

Marty—

Andy Bernat and Nick Matus, who work in the same productivity group in the lighting department, were suspended today by Rhoades, the supervisor. Their suspension begins immediately, pending investigation.

Andy and Nick, responding to dares from the guys, took the third member of their group, Virginia Piper, into the supply room and tried to remove her blouse. She screamed and struggled and ran out to tell Rhoades. As bad as this sounds, it was all part of the traditional congratulations. Virginia had just let it be known that she was engaged. The plan was to try to strip her and throw her in the shower just like the guys do when any of them gets engaged. Virginia has only worked here three weeks, so she didn't know anything about the custom.

I talked with her after the incident at the end of the shift and explained that the men meant no harm and that they really didn't expect to be able to strip her. I told her that they wouldn't even have tried it if they didn't consider her one of the guys and that she shouldn't be upset. I also tried to talk with her about responsibilities to fellow union members who had no intention of hurting her. She believes me but can't believe they'd do that to her. And she thinks Andy and Nick were too rough with her. She said that she won't be pressing any charges with the police and she herself won't pursue anything with management—and wouldn't testify against them—but that she also wouldn't go out of her way to have the matter dropped. She was awfully angry. She has already given a statement to plant security at Rhoades' orders right after the incident; she told me that it was only a few sentences, saying that they tried to take off her blouse.

Rhoades understands the traditional congratulations party very well. There was no need for an immediate suspension—Bernat and Matus aren't any danger to anyone. And Rhoades told them that they may be discharged—that isn't progressive discipline. Besides, his action is based totally on a report; he didn't see anything personally.

I told Nick and Andy to contact you and fill you in completely so that you could file a grievance. Maybe they used bad judgment and should be reprimanded—but certainly not suspended or discharged.

Lenny

Normally you first would talk with the supervisor involved, in this case the lighting department supervisor, J.W. Rhoades. But since Rhoades has already issued the discipline, the grievance will go directly to Dick Robel, the employee relations manager.

At the least, the company will probably accuse Bernat and Matus of horseplay. At the worst, they may be charged with assault or sexual harassment. But management is on thin ice. The "standard parties" are known to supervisors and have been condoned.

Role of the Employee Relations Manager

Your name is Dick Robel. You are employee relations manager at the Quantum Electric Supply Company. You were away from the office on a business trip yesterday and found the following note from Supervisor J.W. Rhoades on your desk this morning, June 12, when you came in.

Mr. Robel:

Shortly after the end of the day shift today, June 11, I suspended Andy Bernat and Nick Matus effective immediately, pending an investigation.

Matus and Bernat work in a three-person productivity group with Virginia Piper, an employee hired only three weeks ago. Just at the end of the shift, she ran into my office, screaming and nearly hysterical, saying that Matus and Bernat had grabbed her in the supply room and tried to take off her blouse. She said that she thought that they were playing some kind of cruel joke—she didn't think that they were trying to rape her or anything—but that they had been rough with her. I told her to go to the security shanty immediately to give a statement and wait for me there.

I then went to the locker room to confront Bernat and Matus, telling them both to come to my office. They came, along with their steward, Lenny Colosimo; a bunch of the men tagged along behind. Apparently they had been dared to give Virginia the standard congratulations party since she had told everyone that she just got engaged. What usually happens when one of the men gets engaged is that they jump him at the end of the shift, strip him, and throw him in the shower.

Frankly, I believe them—I don't think that they meant her any harm and she wasn't hurt in any way. All the men back them up. But I'm still steaming that they'd be stupid and irresponsible enough to pull that stunt with one of the women. And they did seem a little sarcastic to me about what had taken place.

I told them that what they had done was serious and couldn't be tolerated. I think that the immediate suspension was justified and I told them that, following the investigation, they might even be discharged. I also told them that they might want to think about getting a lawyer in case Virginia pressed charges. At the very least, I think that we have to give them a stiff suspension and I believe that we should consider discharge. This was a serious matter.

When I went down to the guard shanty to talk to Virginia again, she had calmed down quite a bit. She did give the guard a statement, but a very short one. She told me that since she didn't think they intended to assault her, she wouldn't press charges with the police. She also said that she wouldn't testify against them for company discipline and wouldn't make any accusations. But she said that she wasn't going to cover up anything either or say that it didn't happen. She asked if she could be transferred to another work group and I told her she would be, effective immediately.

I'm sure that you'll get a grievance from the union. Let me know if you have any questions.

J. W. Rhoades
Lighting Dept. Supervisor

When you get union grievances, they are usually filed by the local president, Martin Lowes. Just to be on the safe side, you decide to consult with Mary Washington, the personnel assistant for equal employment opportunity and affirmative action, and have her participate in all grievance meetings concerning the incident. You'll need to give her a complete report.

Role of the Personnel Assistant for EEO and AA

Your name is Mary Washington, personnel assistant for equal employment opportunity and affirmative action with the Quantum Electric Supply Company. You received a call just a few minutes ago this morning, June 12, from the employee relations manager, Dick Robel. He said that there was an incident in the lighting department yesterday involving two male employees trying to remove the blouse of a female employee as part of a practical joke. Robel said that he'd like to talk with you as soon as possible about the company's position with respect to discrimination contract provisions. You'll be seeing him in just a few minutes.

Additional Relevant Information

ARTICLE XII

....Employees will not be suspended, discharged, or otherwise disciplined except for just cause. Ordinarily, except in the case of major offenses, the standards of progressive discipline will be utilized.

ARTICLE II

No employee shall be discriminated against in employment by the Company, the Union, or any other employee, on the basis of race, color, sex, religion, age, handicap, or national origin.

PLANT RULE 6

Horseplay and gambling during working hours or at any time on company premises are strictly prohibited.

STATEMENT OF VIRGINIA PIPER

At the end of the shift today, the other two members of my productivity group, Nick Matus and Andy Bernat, called me into the supply room. After I went in, they closed the door and one held me while the other tried to take off my blouse.

I screamed and shoved at them and they let me go. I ran to Mr. Rhoades' office to report the incident. I do not believe that they were trying to assault or rape me. But I do believe that they were playing some kind of cruel joke and they were rough with me, although I was not injured.

s/Virginia Piper
Taken by W. P. Whitlock
Plant Security   6/11

Roles

UNION	MANAGEMENT
Chief Steward	Maintenance Supervisor
Union President	General Manager

Role of the Chief Steward

Your name is Sam Snyder. You are chief steward of the union representing the employees of the Atozed Lubrication Products Company. You are also the shop steward for all maintenance employees at the plant.

On May 1 you received a copy of a notice sent by the company to Edgar Harpster, the union president, stating management's intention to contract out janitorial service at the plant effective May 15. The company recently made a major expenditure to install special antislip flooring throughout the plant to prevent accidents, which have been a significant problem because of the nature of the products manufactured. According to the company letter, the current janitorial staff does not have the proper equipment or skills to clean the new floors in the production departments. The company intends to place five employees on permanent layoff and to retain the two most senior janitors for other general cleaning. Harpster has asked for your views on how the union should react.

You are aware that it requires much more time to clean the floors if the cleaning were done with the available manual equipment and that it is not possible to keep the new flooring adequately clean with tools such as brooms and mops. But you think that the company simply should purchase modern electric floor scrubbers or pay the janitors overtime for the extra effort required to clean the floors. Because the new flooring was installed throughout the production departments, a large area is involved, and the company would need to purchase large, industrial scrubbing machines.

You talked with the janitors. They said that they are capable of performing the necessary cleaning, either manually with overtime or with electric scrubbers. The most experienced of the janitors estimated the electric scrubbers could be purchased at a one-time cost of several thousand dollars, plus the cost of supplies.

You responded to the union president, Harpster, that you thought that the union should grieve, even though the contract contains no language limiting the right of management to subcontract. Work has never been contracted before, and you argued that the recognition clause of the contract is an implied limitation on the right of the company to change wages, hours, or terms and conditions of employment unilaterally; the effect of the contracting out is to undermine the bargaining unit. You told Harpster that you'd also check with the international staff representative about the advisability of an unfair labor practice charge.

Role of the Union President

Your name is Edgar Harpster. You are the president of local 2307, the union representing employees of the Atozed Lubrication Products Company, where you work as a machine tender. On May 1, you received a notice from the company informing the union that management intended to eliminate five janitors effective May 15 and to subcontract the work. You asked for the comments of Sam Snyder, the local's chief steward and the shop steward for all maintenance employees.

The company recently made a major expenditure to install special antislip flooring thoughout the plant to prevent accidents, which have been a significant problem because of the nature of the products manufactured. According to the company letter, the current janitorial staff does not have the proper equipment or skills to clean the new floors in the production departments. Management will place five employees on permanent layoff and retain the two most senior janitors for other general cleaning.

Snyder told you that it does require much more time to clean the new floors with only mops and brooms and, in fact, that it's virtually impossible to keep the new flooring clean with manual tools. He talked with the janitors. They said that they could do the job, either manually if paid overtime for the extra time and effort required or using modern electric floor scrubbers if the company would purchase them. A large area is involved, so the company would have to buy large, industrial scrubbing machines. The most experienced janitor estimated that this could be done for several thousand dollars plus the ongoing cost of supplies.

Snyder pointed out that the contract is silent on subcontracting. There is no language limiting management's right to contract out, but it has never been discussed or done before. Snyder argued that the recognition clause of the contract is an implied limitation on the right of the company to change wages, hours, or terms and conditions of employment unilaterally and that the effect of contracting out is to undermine the bargaining unit. He said that he'd also check with the international staff representative about whether an unfair labor practice charge should be filed; he recommended proceeding with the grievance.

You agree with Snyder's appraisal of the situation. The electric floor scrubbers are not expensive, especially compared to the cost of the new flooring. Employees can do the work efficiently if properly equipped. The cost of the equipment would be a one-time expense. You don't see how the company can gain any significant economic savings by the use of outside contractors, at least not enough to justify undercutting the bargaining unit. Besides, the janitors may be used as a stepping stone for other subcontracting.

You decide to file a grievance to protect the rights of the janitors and the union. You file grievances with Donald Taylor, the general manager.

Your name is Glenn Callahan. You are maintenance supervisor for the Atozed Lubrication Products Company. You supervise 48 maintenance employees, including the janitorial staff. During the past year, you also coordinated the introduction of a new safety program at the plant. Among other improvements, the new program involved the installation of expensive antislip flooring throughout the production departments. The new flooring is designed to prevent exactly the kind of dangerous slipping accidents caused by spilled lubricants, which have been common.

The new flooring must be cleaned regularly and thoroughly. Since the floors were installed, you have noticed that the janitors have significant problems cleaning them with the manual tools available. The design of the flooring requires vigorous scrubbing to remove spilled lubricants; the janitors have not been able to clean the regular spills in the alotted time. You recognize that they are making a good effort, but their mops and brooms are just not effective.

You informed the general manager, Donald Taylor, that the floors could be better cleaned by an outside contractor who would bring in the proper electric industrial scrubbing machines. The subcontractor could simply bring in a crew at the end of the shift and thoroughly clean the entire plant. The number of janitors could then be reduced, resulting in a significant savings. You suggested that only two of the seven janitors would have to be retained for general cleaning. Your major concern is with the efficiency of the plant and the safety of the employees.

Taylor told you that he was accepting your suggestion and that the work would be contracted out. He said that he would inform the union by letter today, May 1, and that the work would be contracted out effective May 15. He also congratulated you for the safety program and for your cost-saving suggestion.

Role of the General Manager

Your name is Donald Taylor. You are general manager of the Atozed Lubrication Products Company. During a recent monthly staff meeting, Glenn Callahan, the maintenance supervisor, suggested that much of the janitorial work done at the plant should be subcontracted. Callahan had coordinated the introduction of a new safety program at the plant during the past year, which included purchase and installation of an expensive antislip floor covering throughout the production departments. The new flooring is designed to prevent some of the dangerous slipping accidents, which are almost inevitable since lubricants are constantly being spilled. The new flooring seems to have reduced such accidents significantly.

Callahan reported, however, that the janitors cannot clean the new flooring efficiently with their present manual equipment. Dirty floors, even with the new flooring, still lead to accidents and injuries. While minor spills can be taken care of when they occur, the floors in general need cleaning daily. The janitors, according to Callahan, simply have been accomplishing too little cleaning with too great a disruption in operations. It is not their fault; mops and brooms simply don't work on the new flooring.

You studied Callahan's suggestion and determined that a contractor could be secured to do the work at the end of the shift every day, using large industrial electric scrubbers, at a considerable savings in labor costs. If Atozed purchased the scrubbers itself for use by the janitors, the cost would be about $4,800 plus service contracts on the machines and supplies. But Callahan suggested that five of the seven janitors could be permanently furloughed and only the two senior janitors retained for general cleaning, which would result in a significant savings compared to the cost of contracting out. Subcontracting would also save Callahan from supervising one group among the 48 employees for whom he is responsible, freeing him for other responsibilities. Although Atozed has never contracted out work before, the labor agreement is entirely silent on the issue. Clearly you would be acting in the best interest of the company from both financial and safety considerations; subcontracting would be a justifiable exercise of management rights.

You decided to accept Callahan's suggestion and complimented him for it. Today, May 1, you sent a letter to the president of union local 2307, Edgar Harpster, informing the union of management's decision to subcontract effective May 15 and of the permanent layoff of the five most junior janitors. In the letter you justified the decision on the fact that the current employees do not have the skills or the equipment to clean the new floors properly.

Additional Relevant Information

ARTICLE I RECOGNITION
The Company recognizes the Union as the sole and exclusive bargaining agent for employees in the certified bargaining unit.

ARTICLE VI MANAGEMENT RIGHTS
The Company possesses the right to manage all operations, including the direction of the work force, and the right to plan, direct, and control the operation of all facilities and property except as modified by this Agreement. The listing of specific rights is not intended as a waiver of any management rights not listed and not specifically surrendered.

Roles

UNION	MANAGEMENT

Chief Shop Steward
One or Two Shop
    Committee Members
	Director of
	    Employee Relations
	One or Two Managers or
	    Supervisors

Background

On September 1 the director of employee relations, James T. Farrell, posted on all official bulletin boards a notice that the company reserved its right to question and call as witnesses employees who knew of any work-related wrongdoing and that refusal to answer questions or testify would lead to disciplinary action. The company was experiencing a significant theft problem.

NOTICE

The comptroller is investigating employees concerning potentially serious cases of theft of company property.

All employees are hereby notified that the company reserves its right to question and to call as witnesses in legal or company disciplinary proceedings any employees who may know of work-related wrongdoing.

Employees called for questioning who refuse to answer or to testify will be liable for disciplinary action.

James T. Farrell
Director of Employee Relations

Date: September 1
Distribution: All official bulletin boards

On September 3, after a shop committee meeting to discuss the company's notice, the local 342 Chief Shop Steward, Alfred Alfiero, posted a response on the bulletin board reserved for the union's use.

! W A R N I N G !

The Shop Committee of Local 342 believes the September 1 company notice threatening disciplinary action for employees who refuse to cooperate in interrogations concerning the conduct of other employees represents gross and unwarranted intimidation.

We believe that any disciplinary action following a refusal to answer questions would be a violation of our contract and our Constitutional rights.

Since the company has threatened disciplinary action for refusal to cooperate, we urge all bargaining unit members *not* to participate in any way without first demanding the presence of a union steward. The local leadership is requesting an immediate meeting with the company and demands that the company withdraw its notice.

Alfred Alfiero
Chief Shop Steward

Date: September 3

Approximately two hours after the posting of the response from Alfiero, a representative from Farrell's office, acting on his instructions, removed the union's notice from the bulletin board. Upon receiving a report that the notice had been removed, Alfiero notified Farrell's office of the union's intent to file a grievance and demanded an immediate meeting to discuss it at step 3.

Relevant Contract Provisions

ARTICLE XXXIV UNION BUSINESS

Section 1. The Company agrees to provide space on a bulletin board to the Union for the announcement of meetings, election of officers, and any other material related to Union business. The Union shall not post material detrimental to the labor-management relationship nor of a political or controversial nature.

ARTICLE II MANAGEMENT RIGHTS

Section 1. It is understood and agreed that the Company, at its sound discretion, possesses the right, in accordance with applicable laws, to manage all operations including the direction of the working force and the right to plan, direct, and control the operation of all equipment and other property of the Company, except as modified by this Agreement. The Company retains all inherent management rights except those specifically modified in this Agreement.

ARTICLE XXIX DISCHARGE AND DISCIPLINE

Section 1. The Company shall not discharge, suspend, or otherwise discipline any employee without just cause.

ARTICLE XXXIX GRIEVANCES

Section 1. Any grievance or dispute that may arise concerning the meaning or interpretation of the Agreement shall be settled in the following manner.

    Step I. The employee, alone or accompanied by a Union steward, or the Union, shall present the grievance orally to the immediate supervisor within 10 days of the event giving rise to it. The supervisor shall attempt to resolve the matter and shall announce his decision within 7 days.

Step II. If the grievance is not settled at Step I, the grievance must be presented in writing to the Department Manager within 7 days of the supervisor's response. The Department Manager shall investigate and respond in writing within 7 days of receipt of the grievance.

Step III. If the grievance is not settled at Step II, the grievance shall be appealed to the Director of Employee Relations within 7 days of the Department Manager's response. The Director of Employee Relations shall investigate and respond in writing within 10 days of receipt of the grievance.

Section 2. Notwithstanding any other provision of this Article, a grievance shall be presented at the lowest Step at which the Company official has authority to settle the grievance.

Roles

UNION	MANAGEMENT
Union President, the Grievant One or Two Shop Committee Members	Production Supervisor Manager, Personnel and Labor Relations

Role of the Union President

Your name is Merle Blue. You are president of local union 2611 of the United Food Processors. You are employed as a quality control inspector by Tri-State Foods Company, which prepares packaged meals and food items for use in cafeterias and vending machines.

As a result of local negotiations last year, the company and union agreed to undertake a job enrichment program, which has gone relatively well. The program began a little over five months ago. It includes human relations training for supervisors, work group leaders, and quality circles that participate in setting work group objectives and suggesting changes in production methods.

You told the company during the negotiations that you were suspicious of their motivation but you would agree to participate in and promote the program if the agreement were ratified. It was approved, but you took a lot of heat for cooperating too much with management, both from rank and filers and from other area union presidents. To get the support of your members, you had to return to management and modify the agreement so that the enrichment program was only experimental for six months and would be fully evaluated before any extension. The company agreed to the change. The labor relations climate, which had been bad, seems to have improved at Tri-State, but the acid test is negotiations for the new contract, which begin July 6, in three weeks.

While punching out yesterday afternoon, you received a letter from Paul Kennedy, manager of personnel and labor relations, explaining that all employees were being given an evaluation questionnaire concerning the experimental job enrichment program. The cover letter points out that the company and union agreed to evaluate the program before any decision to extend it. The letter also emphasizes that the questionnaire is anonymous and asks for 100 percent participation in filling out the form. The questionnaire was attached. At the top of the cover letter was a note handwritten to you from Kennedy.

Merle—

FYI. We've worked up this evaluation form and will distribute it in the time card slots tomorrow morning. All foremen have been instructed to give employees a 30-minute break at the beginning of the shift to fill it out. Foremen will collect the forms by having them folded once and then deposited in a large box to insure anonymity. Assuming that you have no objection, I'll have our secretaries tabulate the responses and—probably in a day or two—we'll share the complete results, including the forms if you want them. Then we can see where we want to go with the program.

P.K.

You put the letter and questionnaire in your lunchbox, a little relieved that you didn't have to worry about putting together an evaluation questionnaire but also a little disturbed that it hadn't been shared with you earlier. After supper before reading the paper, you looked over the questionnaire.

You hadn't read many questions before you became incensed. It was clear to you that the questions went beyond the program and requested information for bargaining purposes. You tried to call Kennedy, but his wife said that he was traveling on business and couldn't be reached until he returned the day after tomorrow. You then called as many stewards as you could to tell them to instruct their people not to answer the questionnaire until you had a chance to straighten things out. You arrived at work 30 minutes early this morning to post this sign on the union bulletin board located near the time clock.

LOCAL 2611 MEMBERS!

DO NOT fill out the questionnaire to be distributed by foremen this morning. The union was not consulted and it may be used unfairly by the company in negotiations.

Merle Blue, President

Production Supervisor John McConnell saw the notice as employees were punching in and immediately sought you out. He said that you could post only material concerning union business and could not direct employees to refuse to answer the questionnaire. He told you to remove the notice immediately, but you refused. He then reminded you that the notice itself was insubordinate and that you also were being insubordinate in refusing to remove it. He again ordered you, and you refused. He told you that you were suspended for the rest of the day and that you should appear in Kennedy's office tomorrow morning.

McConnell then went to the time clock area to remove the notice himself. In the meantime, however, employees had crumpled the surveys, thrown most in the waste cans, and scattered some on the floor. McConnell was enraged and told you as you were leaving that he'd recommend severe discipline.

You've decided to use the day preparing a grievance to hand to Kennedy tomorrow morning and consulting the international. Your meeting in Kennedy's office is scheduled for 9 tomorrow. You've also asked several shop committee members to accompany you tomorrow and to meet tonight after dinner to talk about strategy.

Role of the Production Supervisor

Your name is John McConnell. You are production supervisor at the Tri-State Foods Company, where you've worked for six years. Tri-State prepares packaged meals and food items for use in cafeterias and vending machines.

This morning you went to the time clock area as usual just before employees began arriving and, while drinking your coffee, noticed a sign on the union bulletin board directing employees not to answer a questionnaire on the experimental job enrichment program, which foremen were instructed to distribute this morning.

LOCAL 2611 MEMBERS!

DO NOT fill out the questionnaire to be distributed by foremen this morning. The union was not consulted and it may be used unfairly by the company in negotiations.

Merle Blue, President

The experimental program, emphasizing human relations training and quality circles, was ending after six months. The company and union had agreed to it in the last negotiations and had also agreed to evaluate the program before a decision about extending it. Paul Kennedy, manager of personnel and labor relations, had developed the questionnaire; you and he had worked out the best way to distribute it.

The plans were to distribute them in the time card slots this morning along with a cover letter from Kennedy emphasizing that union and management had agreed to evaluate the program, reminding employees that the questionnaire would be anonymous, and asking for 100 percent participation. You had a meeting with all foremen yesterday to explain the procedure. There was to be a 30-minute break at the beginning of the shift for completing the questionnaire. Foremen then were to collect them after employees had folded the forms once and place them in large boxes to ensure anonymity. Kennedy is out of town until tomorrow and left you in charge of the evaluation arrangements. Once collected, the forms were to be given to Kennedy's secretary for tabulation.

You were angered by such obvious insubordination and immediately sought out Merle Blue, finding him near his work station in quality control. You told him that the notice was insubordinate and that the union could use the bulletin board only for union business. You ordered him to remove it immediately, but he refused, heatedly. You were angry about his attitude and language and again ordered him, reminding him that the notice itself was insubordinate and that he was also if he didn't remove it. He again refused. You ordered him home for the rest of the day and told him to appear in Kennedy's office tomorrow morning.

You then returned to the time clock area to remove the notice yourself. In the meantime, however, the word (obviously) had spread because employees had crumpled the questionnaires and scattered them on the floor.

Even more angered, you told Blue as he was leaving that you'd be recommending severe discipline. You then told foremen to forget the questionnaires since the employees had thrown them away.

Taking the union notice from the bulletin board, you carried it to Kennedy's office and gave it to his secretary, asking her to tell him that the survey was not done and that you had suspended Blue for insubordination. You told her that Blue would be in at 9 tomorrow and asked her to have Kennedy talk with you to get the details in advance.

Role of the Manager, Personnel and Labor Relations

Your name is Paul Kennedy. You have been manager, personnel and labor relations, for the Tri-State Foods Company for two years. Tri-State prepares packaged meals and food items for use in cafeterias and vending machines. It is organized by the United Food Processors, local union 2611.

Labor relations were in a relatively bad state when you were hired. One of your primary responsibilities has been improving them. The task wasn't made any easier by the company's increasing difficulty in competing; you also were required to improve productivity. In your first contract negotiations, you convinced the union to agree to a job enrichment program, which involves human relations training for supervisors, work group leaders, and quality circles. Things seem to have improved.

The union president, Merle Blue, was suspicious of your motivation for the program from the beginning but agreed to try it in the last negotiations. He took a lot of heat for the program from rank-and-file members charging that he was being too cooperative with management. As a result, he had to return to the table to seek a modification in the job enrichment program. It had to be experimental, for six months only, and subject to a complete evaluation before any extension. You had no problems with that change, so the company agreed. You've had experience with these programs and always have been confident that the program could improve labor relations and productivity and that, given a fair test, the workers would support it.

Since the six months are nearly over, you took the initiative of developing a questionnaire for all employees in order to gain agreed evaluation. You also wrote a cover letter explaining that the union and company agreed to evaluate the experimental program and that the questionnaire would be completed anonymously; you asked for candor and 100 percent cooperation. You then worked out with John McConnell, production supervisor, a distribution system, which involved putting the questionnaires and cover letters in the time card slots at the beginning of a shift and letting all the employees have a 30-minute break to complete them. Foremen would then collect the forms in large boxes after they'd been folded once to ensure anonymity; your secretarial staff would then tabulate the results, after which they and the original forms would be shared with the union.

The plan seemed efficient. You thought that it would be appreciated by Merle Blue, the union president, since the union wouldn't have to do any work in developing the questonnaire or tabulating the results. You're certain that the program will be evaluated highly by the employees. Since the results will be tabulated only three weeks before new contract talks start July 6, establishing the attitude of successful cooperation is sure to help the negotiations. The forms were to have been distributed under John McConnell's supervision yesterday while you were away on business. Before you left two days ago, you put a copy of the form and cover letter in Merle Blue's time card slot and wrote a personal note explaining the procedure that would be followed.

You were looking forward to returning to the office this morning to read the tabulated results. Instead, you were surprised and disturbed to learn from your secretary that McConnell had left a message that the forms weren't distributed yesterday. According to the message, Merle Blue had posted a notice telling employees not to complete the questionnaire and they had thrown the forms away upon punching in. McConnell suspended Blue for a day for posting the notice and for refusing to remove it. The notice was attached to the message.

LOCAL 2611 MEMBERS!

DO NOT fill out the questionnaire to be distributed by foremen this morning. The union was not consulted and it may be used unfairly by the company in negotiations.

Merle Blue, President

The message from McConnell also said that he wanted to fill you in on the details and that Blue had been ordered to appear in your office at 9 this morning.

Naturally you're upset. The union bulletin board is for union business only. You're not about to have the union president directing employees to disobey management directives. That's as clear a case of insubordination as you've seen. More important, everything that's been accomplished is threatened. The questions in no way undermined the union for bargaining; they were directed at an evaluation of the experimental program that had been agreed jointly. You feel that you've been sandbagged by Blue and that this may be just the opening round of negotiations tactics. You don't know why and you've had no hints—maybe the problem is union politics and Blue isn't in control—but you're afraid that the negotiations could go badiy. You'll want to talk with McConnell before the meeting with Blue.

LETTER AND QUESTIONNAIRE

Dear Tri-State Employee:

Tri-State Foods and Local Union 2611 agreed in the last contract to the experimental job enrichment program in which we all have participated for almost six months. The Union and Company also agreed to evaluate the program before making any decision to extend it.

Attached is a questionnaire concerning the job enrichment program, asking you to respond to important issues of quality-of-work life and productivity at Tri-State under the program. You will be given an extended 30-minute break at the beginning of the shift today to complete the questionnaire.

In order to provide an effective measure of the program, please answer the questions honestly. The questionnaire will be anonymous. Please answer all questions—we need 100 percent cooperation for an accurate evaluation. When finished, fold the form in half and deposit it in the collection box, which your foreman will provide. All tabulated results and the completed, anonymous, questionnaires will be shared immediately with the Union.

Thank you for your cooperation,

Paul Kennedy, Manager
Personnel and Labor Relations

JOB ENRICHMENT PROGRAM EVALUATION

1. Do you feel that you can communicate effectively with your supervisor?

2. Do you feel that your supervisor is more responsive now to your views and suggestions?

3. Do you believe the job enrichment program has given you greater independence in making decisions on the job? Please explain.

4. Do you believe the job enrichment program has provided you with additional job responsibilities? Please explain.

5. Do you find that your work has become more rewarding under the job enrichment program? Please explain.

6. Do you feel that you should receive additional compensation for your work under the job enrichment program? Please explain.

7. Do you believe that the job enrichment program has led to increased productivity. Please explain.

8. Do you feel that the Company has rewarded you adequately for the work experience and knowledge that you have brought to the job enrichment program? Please explain.

9. Do you feel that your work has become more interesting under the job enrichment program? Please explain.

10. Do you feel that the job enrichment program has increased your knowledge of other people's jobs? Please explain.

11. Do you feel that job trading within your work group would increase your job satisfaction? Please explain.

12. Do you feel that additional job satisfaction will develop if the job enrichment program is extended? Please explain.

Please add any other comments. Thank you for your help.

CASE 14: OLD COFFEE GROUNDS?

Roles

UNION	MANAGEMENT
Local 1423 President	Employee Relations Manager
One or Two Grievance	One or Two Other Managers
Committee Members	or Supervisors

Background

On September 15, members of local 1423 ratified a new contract with the Maximillian Medical Supply Company. The new agreement, which took effect October 1, was reached only after a bitter four-week strike. During negotiations, management charged that poor employee attitudes had led to a decline in productivity, which threatened the company's ability to remain competitive. The company demanded that employees pay greater attention to efficient production under the new contract.

On October 5 Maximillian Supply sent a letter to all employees informing them that drinking coffee during working hours, except during official breaks, would be prohibited, effective October 7. Notices were also posted, and the union was notified officially. The company letter charged that time spent drinking coffee on the job had reduced productivity and contributed to poor employee attitudes.

Nothing had been said at negotiations specifically concerning coffee drinking; no contract language had ever referred to it in any way. For as long as anyone could remember, employees routinely drank coffee from their own thermos bottles as they wished, as long as they remained at their work stations and continued working. About 10 years ago a coffee club had been formed; nearly all coffee drinkers were members, including many supervisors. The club collected regular contributions toward the purchase of paper cups, plastic stirs, sugar, and powdered creamer; the supplies were kept in an old drug cabinet that the company had provided. Coffee itself was not purchased; employees had to bring their own. On October 6, the company posted a notice on the supplies cabinet, which said that the supplies could be used only on official breaks, effective October 7, and that they could not be replaced once they were depleted.

No one had ever been disciplined for leaving a work station briefly to use the supplies or for drinking coffee while working, although occasionally an employee was warned about malingering around the supply cabinet. The company was small, set up in an old warehouse. The atmosphere had been close, easygoing, and friendly until the last year, when business conditions began to decline rapidly. The earlier "family" atmosphere contributed to the bitterness of the strike, when an agreement was not reached after the initial negotiations.

Arguing that no agreement, including the new one, had ever mentioned coffee drinking, the president of the local notified the company that he would be filing a grievance on behalf of all employees. The grievance would contend that coffee drinking was a past practice that management could not alter except through negotiation with the union. The employee relations manager told the local president to go ahead and file the grievance. He said that as a matter of management rights and as a result of Article XXIII, which was new in the recently ratified contract, the company could prohibit coffee drinking on the job during working time.

Relevant Contract Provisions

ARTICLE VI MANAGEMENT RIGHTS

The Company retains all rights to manage the business except those specifically surrendered in this agreement.

ARTICLE XXIII TOTALITY OF AGREEMENT

This Agreement takes precedence over all prior agreements and supercedes them in every way, including all understandings and practices, whether oral or written. The total understandings between the parties are represented by the Agreement.

CASE 15: A MISSED OPPORTUNITY

Roles

UNION	MANAGEMENT
Grievant	Tin Plate Department
Grievance Committee	Supervisor
Chairman	Labor Relations Manager

Role of the Grievant

Your name is Peter Evankovich. You are a craneman in the tin plate department, a job that you've worked for the last 5 years of your 12 years with the Mackintosh Steel Company. When the schedule was posted on December 20 for Christmas week, you were scheduled to work your usual assignment, crane 10, on Sunday (23), Thursday (27), Friday (28), and Saturday (29). Monday (24) and Tuesday (25) are recognized holidays in the contract, and you were scheduled to have them off as paid holidays.

In the tin plate department, where you work, incumbent cranemen pick their preferred cranes by seniority and then receive assignments on those cranes to the extent that turns are available according to the work to be done. If less than five turns are available, cranemen are scheduled, if possible, on other cranes, which they can operate in order to reach a five-turn schedule, but they may not displace incumbents on those cranes. Crane laborers are then scheduled to operate cranes in order to fill in for vacations or other anticipated vacancies and to prevent overtime (more than five turns assigned in a week) from occurring for the regular cranemen. This scheduling procedure has been the practice for at least the five years that you've worked as a craneman and the three years before that, when you were a crane laborer.

You noticed on the schedule that four crane laborers were scheduled on the three shifts during Christmas week, including two on your scheduled shift. All of the crane laborers were scheduled for four turns that week. Among the cranemen, three others were scheduled for four turns on the various shifts and four were scheduled for five turns, according to the work requiring their cranes. On Tuesday, when you were scheduled for a holiday, and Wednesday, when you were scheduled to be off, a crane laborer, Mark Malenson, was scheduled to operate crane 18 on your shift. You have operated 18 in the past. You concluded that the schedule forced you to miss an opportunity for a fifth scheduled turn, which you should get according to the established practice. You asked the tin plate supervisor, James Hawkins, why you were not scheduled for a fifth turn on either Tuesday or Wednesday. He checked with the schedule clerk and then told you that you were not permitted to work another turn that week by filling in on another crane because it would involve overtime.

You believe that you should get your fifth turn before any crane laborer is scheduled and contacted the zone committeeman, Lee Presti, to file a grievance. Presti agreed with your version of the practice and said that he'd write a report to Tommy O'Halloran, the committee chairman, for filing immediately at step 2 because of the short time remaining before the week starts.

Role of the Grievance Committee Chairman

Your name is Tommy O'Halloran. You are grievance committee chairman of the local union representing the employees of the Mackintosh Steel Company. Just before noon today, December 20, you received the following report from Zone Committeeman Lee Presti.

Tommy—

I have a grievance concerning scheduling during Christmas week, which will have to be filed immediately because of the timing.

Peter Evankovich, a craneman in the tin plate department, believes that he is missing an opportunity to work five turns because a crane laborer has been improperly scheduled to work an assignment that Evankovich should have according to past practice. I agree.

There is a clear scheduling practice for cranemen in the tin plate department, which has been operating for years and is even referred to in the 1965 memorandum of understanding. The practice was being followed even before it was officially recognized in the 1965 local agreements.

The practice is that incumbent cranemen pick their preferred cranes according to seniority and then receive assignments on those cranes to the extent turns are available in any week. If less than five turns are available, cranemen are scheduled, if possible, on other cranes, which they can operate in order to reach a five turn schedule but they may not displace an incumbent on another crane. Crane laborers are scheduled to fill in for vacations or other anticipated vacancies and to prevent overtime by ensuring that cranemen are not scheduled for more than five turns.

On the schedule for Christmas week, Evankovich is scheduled for turns on Sunday (23), Thursday (27), Friday (28), and Saturday (29) and for days off on paid holiday on Monday (24) and Tuesday (25), the holidays recognized in the contract. He regularly operates crane 10, which is scheduled for only four turns that week.

However, a crane laborer, Mark Malenson, is scheduled to work four turns that week including Tuesday and Wednesday on crane 18. Evankovich has worked crane 18. He should be scheduled for a fifth turn before any crane laborer is assigned to a crane that Evankovich can operate.

When Evankovich questioned the tin plate supervisor, James Hawkins, about why he didn't have a fifth turn on either Tuesday or Wednesday in place of Malenson, he was told that he couldn't work another turn that week by filling in on another crane because it would involve overtime.

It is true that the company can schedule crane laborers to avoid giving cranemen overtime—the 1965 memo even recognizes that. The contract is clear that no one is entitled to overtime.

But the company cannot violate past practice this way. The point is that we're not grieving for *overtime* but only for the five scheduled turns to which Evankovich is entitled if they are available. While overtime might ultimately result at some later part of the week, that would merely be the effect of following the established practice. The contract mandates that overtime must be paid beyond five regular working days.

Therefore, we must make clear that we are not seeking entitlement to overtime but entitlement to a fifth scheduled working turn. The company will probably try to make it out to be a grievance seeking overtime, which they can easily reject. We can't let the practice, which is longstanding, be undermined that way.

Lee

At step 2, you file grievances with the labor relations manager, Gerald Dopler.

Role of the Tin Plate Department Supervisor

Your name is James Hawkins. You are supervisor of the tin plate department of the Mackintosh Steel Company. This afternoon, December 20, you were asked by the secretary to Gerald Dopler, the labor relations manager, to write a memo describing the scheduling practice for cranemen in your department as quickly as possible. He also asked for your views on a grievance about to be filed by Peter Evankovich, a craneman seeking a fifth scheduled working turn next week, Christmas week.

You had posted the schedule earlier this morning; it didn't take long for Evankovich to question it. You assumed that he would file a grievance. In response to Dopler's request, you prepared and submitted the following memo.

Subject: Scheduling in Tin Plate
Possible Craneman Grievance

The standard practice for scheduling tin plate cranemen has been in place for years, since at least the early 1960s. It is as follows.

1. Incumbent cranemen pick their cranes by seniority and receive assignments on those cranes to the extent that turns are available.

2. If less than five turns are available, cranemen are scheduled on other cranes, which they can operate up to five turns except that they may not displace incumbents on other cranes.

3. Crane laborers are used to fill in vacancies and to prevent scheduled overtime among the regular cranemen.

With respect to the potential grievance, it has no foundation. The above practice was followed in scheduling Evankovich for Christmas week. His crane, 10, is scheduled to work only four turns, Sunday (12/23), Thursday (12/27), Friday (12/28), and Saturday (12/29). He is also scheduled for paid holidays on Monday (12/24) and Tuesday (12/25), the holidays recognized in the contract.

All other cranes have incumbents working on Monday, Tuesday, and Wednesday, except 18, where I have scheduled Malenson, a crane laborer, on Tuesday and Wednesday.

Although Evankovich would otherwise be eligible to operate 18 for his fifth turn, he is not eligible to displace Malenson because that would result in overtime, or rather *more* overtime for Evankovich. He is already going to be paid for *six* days that week because of the holidays—the four days he is scheduled to work plus the two holidays. He certainly has no right to a *seventh* day (Wednesday) or to double time and a half, which he'd get if he worked Tuesday, a holiday.

The union will claim that according to the practice Evankovich should get five turns before any crane laborer is assigned to a crane that he can operate. That's exactly correct *except* that they fail to recognize that he has no entitlement to the overtime that he is seeking and he is already scheduled to be paid not for just five days but for six.

James Hawkins

Role of the Labor Relations Manager

Your name is Gerald Dopler, labor relations manager of the Mackintosh Steel Company. Earlier this afternoon, December 20, you were notified by Tommy O'Halloran, the union's grievance committee chairman, that the union wants an immediate step 2 meeting to discuss a potential grievance concerning the Christmas week schedule for a craneman in the tin plate department, Peter Evankovich. You told your secretary to ask the tin plate superintendent, James Hawkins, to submit a memo describing tin plate scheduling practices and commenting on the potential Evankovich grievance as quickly as possible. Your secretary just brought in his memo.

Subject: Scheduling in Tin Plate
          Possible Craneman Grievance

The standard practice for scheduling tin plate cranemen has been in place for years, since at least the early 1960s. It is as follows.

1. Incumbent cranemen pick their cranes by seniority and receive assignments on those cranes to the extent that turns are available.

2. If less than five turns are available, cranemen are scheduled on other cranes, which they can operate up to five turns except that they may not displace incumbents on other cranes.

3. Crane laborers are used to fill in vacancies and to prevent scheduled overtime among the regular cranemen.

With respect to the potential grievance, it has no foundation. The above practice was followed in scheduling Evankovich for Christmas week. His crane, 10, is scheduled to work only four turns, Sunday (12/23), Thursday (12/27), Friday (12/28), and Saturday (12/29). He is also scheduled for paid holidays on Monday (12/24) and Tuesday (12/25), the holidays recognized in the contract.

All other cranes have incumbents working on Monday, Tuesday, and Wednesday, except 18, where I have scheduled Malenson, a crane laborer, on Tuesday and Wednesday.

Although Evankovich would otherwise be eligible to operate 18 for his fifth turn, he is not eligible to displace Malenson because that would result in overtime, or rather *more* overtime for Evankovich. He is already going to be paid for *six* days that week because of the holidays—the four days he is scheduled to work plus the two holidays. He certainly has no right to a *seventh* day (Wednesday) or to double time and a half which he'd get if he worked Tuesday, a holiday.

The union will claim that according to the practice, Evankovich should get five turns before any crane laborer is assigned to a crane that he can operate. That's exactly correct *except* that they fail to recognize that he has no entitlement to the overtime that he is seeking and he is already scheduled to be paid not just for 5 days but for six.

James Hawkins

Hawkins has done a masterful job analyzing the grievance. You may want to keep an eye on him for future opportunities. The situation seems clear: the contract, the practice, and even the 1965 memorandum of understanding, which the union will no doubt trot out, all recognize the company's right to schedule so as to avoid overtime. The union has just found a way to take this scheduling practice and, with a little razzle-dazzle, make it appear that Evankovich is entitled to overtime.

Actually, you can't understand why the union would grieve. The union members know very well that they can't grieve for overtime entitlement. You'll have to wait to see what O'Halloran has to say. But it looks like this one will be a short grievance meeting—and a short response.

Additional Relevant Information

ARTICLE III

The management of the plant and the direction of the work force, including the right to hire, transfer, schedule, suspend, or discharge for proper cause, discipline, and assign work, is vested exclusively in the Company.

ARTICLE XII

A. No provision of this Agreement concerning the normal hours of work, nor any practice concerning scheduling of the normal hours of work, shall be construed as a guarantee of hours of work per day or per week. Nor shall any provision or practice concerning the calculation of payment for work or for overtime compensation or any other compensation be construed as a guarantee of hours of work per day or per week.

K. Recognized holidays, whether worked or not and whether scheduled as a day of work or not, shall be counted as a day worked in determining eligibility for overtime.

S. Notwithstanding any other provision of this Agreement, the decision to schedule overtime is solely the right of the Company. Overtime work will be offered in accordance with the relevant provisions of the Agreement if any apply.

EXCERPT FROM 1965 MEMORANDUM OF UNDERSTANDING

7. The Union requested that incumbents should have first preference to work on their jobs except where overtime would be involved and that incumbents of the established seniority unit should have preference on work in the unit except where overtime would be involved. The Company responded that this has been and continues to be the Company's policy except where overtime would be involved, or an emergency exists, or some other liability, such as short week SUB benefits, would be incurred.

Roles

UNION	MANAGEMENT
Grievant	Director, Personnel and
Shop Steward	Labor Relations
	Personnel Representative

Background

On March 1 Charles Bingham, lead mechanic in the facilities department of the Brunswick truck body plant, retired after 22 years with the company. Charlie was an excellent employee, liked by all his coworkers, and liked and respected by management. In 22 years, he'd been off sick only twice.

When Bingham retired, three mechanics were on temporary layoff due to a lengthy period of poor business conditions. One mechanic was working a four-day week and one other mechanic was working a five-day week. Ken McCreary, the most senior mechanic next to Bingham, believed that he would be the new lead mechanic. McCreary was fully qualified for the position and was working the five-day week.

The company did not declare a vacancy for lead mechanic, since so few mechanics were employed, and therefore did not post a bid notice for the job. On behalf of McCreary, the union notified the company that it would file a grievance claiming that the company violated the collective bargaining agreement when it did not declare a vacancy for lead mechanic.

Relevant Contract Provisions

ARTICLE XXII POSTING AND BIDDING FOR VACANCIES

A. All vacancies will be offered to the senior qualified bidder in the shop where the vacancy exists regardless of the employee's shift assignment at the time that the vacancy occurs.

B. There shall be an overall ratio of at least 1 lead mechanic to each 7 mechanics in the work force and at no time will a single lead mechanic be responsible for more than 12 mechanics.

C. When a mechanic is on duty alone at a work station, facility, or unit, he shall receive lead mechanic pay for those hours he works alone.

D. No foreman or supervisor shall perform bargaining unit work at any time.

Roles

	UNION	MANAGEMENT

UNION

Grievant
Grievance Committee
  Chairman

MANAGEMENT

Supervisor
Personnel Director

Role of the Grievant

Your name is Frank Carney. You are employed as a warehouseman for the Post Distribution Company. You've worked for Post since 1969 and have been a warehouseman since 1972. Post receives magazines, back issue periodicals, and paperback books from publishing houses and then markets them in bookstores, specialty stores, supermarkets, and newsstands for sale to the public at discount.

You work alongside Jack Hale, a bargaining unit member who has been with Post since 1976. Hale does exactly the same job as you do, but he is also a working foreman, one of two on your shift. He doesn't supervise you or anyone else but is responsible for coordinating the work to be done. His primary responsibility is warehousing, just like yours.

About a month ago, the company installed a small computer terminal in the warehouse to track shipments and count inventories. Inventory control already had programmed in the current stock and the inventory control director gave you, Hale, and your counterparts on the other shift a four-hour orientation on how to use the terminal. You and Jack were told by the supervisor, Norman King, to begin to use the new computer system and to shift over from manual inventory practices as rapidly as you could become comfortable with the machine.

Both you and Jack are learning, but he prefers the terminal much more than you. Apparently he has some familiarity with computers since his son is some sort of computer wizard in school. He began using it faster—but he had to, since he has the other demands on his time as a working foreman. You're nervous about the machine, knowing nothing about computers, but you're picking it up as fast as you have time. When Hale has to perform working foreman duties, you have to handle all the work and at least you know how to do it manually without making some costly mistake.

This morning, August 8, you received the following notice from Personnel in your card slot upon punching in.

> Due to recent economic conditions, the Post Company has been forced to reduce man-hours in the warehouse as well as in other departments. We regret to inform you that, effective August 15, you will be placed on temporary furlough until conditions improve.

You were upset about getting the layoff notice. When you talked with Hale to commiserate and discovered that he hadn't been furloughed, you went through the roof. You are senior to him, and the contract says that layoff is determined by seniority.

You contacted your zone committeeman, Mary Hudak, who said that she'd notify the supervisor, Norman King, that the union would be grieving. Mary said that she'd inform the committee chairman, Steve Sandusky, and that you should see him as soon as possible to talk about filing a written grievance.

Role of the Grievance Committee Chairman

Your name is Stephen Sandusky. You are employed by the Post Distribution Company and are chairman of the union grievance committee. Post receives back issue periodicals, magazines, and paperback books from publishers and then markets them to bookstores, supermarkets, and newsstands for sale at discount.

You received the following note from Mary Hudak, zone committeeman, a few minutes ago this afternoon, August 8.

Steve—

Frank Carney in the warehouse told me this morning that he was being laid off and that Jack Hale, a working foreman in the warehouse, was being retained. Frank is the senior employee, and Jack Hale should be laid off first.

Article 7 says that layoff will be in order of seniority. Hale does the same work as Carney except that he coordinates work and must answer to management for any problems on the shift. He doesn't supervise Frank or anyone else. As a working foreman, he's listed on the plant-wide seniority list but is not included on the warehouseman list.

Frank is just as qualified as Jack. They do the same job, and Frank is more senior. If a working foreman is still needed after the furlough, Frank could do it as easily as Jack.

I think that Frank has a strong case. Surely we never intended that working foremen would have super seniority, did we? I've notified their supervisor, Norman King, that we'll be grieving. Carney will see you shortly to give you the details.

Mary

Role of the Supervisor

You are Norman King, a supervisor at the Post Distribution Company. Post receives magazines, back issue periodicals, and paperback books from publishing houses and then markets them at discount in bookstores, specialty stores, supermarkets, and newsstands.

Inventory turnover is high in such a business. It's essential to know what stock is on hand and to have materials inventoried, stored, and shipped to the distribution centers as rapidly as orders can be processed.

Recently, at the direction of Carl Shaffer, the personnel director, employees in the warehouse were trained in the use of computer terminals, which the company just installed. On instructions from Shaffer, all supervisors, including you, were told to direct employees to cease manual operations and switch over to computer processing of inventories as rapidly as possible.

You supervise the warehouse and several other departments. Business conditions are bad. Within the past week, at a meeting of the supervisors and the personnel director, the decision was made to furlough several people. In the warehouse, your recommendation, concurred in by the personnel director, was to lay off Frank Carney. He received his notice this morning, August 8.

The decision to furlough Carney wasn't easy. He is the least senior person on the warehouseman list but more senior than Jack Hale, a working foreman who does the same job in the Warehouse and will not be furloughed. Working foremen are in the bargaining unit; they do not supervise other employees but simply coordinate work to be done. They have plantwide seniority but are not listed on any department lists because their coordinating responsibilities may span several departments on any given shift.

The contract does not require strict adherence to seniority in layoff; you don't believe that Carney is as qualified as Hale. Following installation of the terminal in the warehouse, you watched both Carney and Hale do their jobs. Hale took to the computer as if second nature to him; he has saved significant time from his warehouse responsibilities, which can be devoted to coordination duties as working foreman. (His son is some sort of computer wizard in school.)

Carney, on the other hand, seems scared by the terminal and has been reluctant to use it from the beginning. He continues to process most orders manually. He is picking it up, slowly, but he's not prepared to begin operating the whole department's inventory and shipping records by computer, which he'd have to do if he remained. Hale is simply more qualified. Besides, you will probably want to keep a working foreman; Carney doesn't have the temperament. Even if he were interested, you wouldn't want him.

At least the company had the foresight to get the computer. You'll be able to keep operating during the layoff even with fewer people, but you can't afford to have a warehouseman who can't handle the computer.

Mary Hudak, the union's zone committeeman, has just informed you that the union will file a grievance on behalf of Carney. You'd better let Shaffer, the personnel director, know that he can expect a grievance from Steve Sandusky, the union's grievance committee chairman.

Role of the Personnel Director

Your name is Carl Shaffer. You are personnel director at the Post Distribution Company. Post receives magazines, back issue periodicals, and paperback books from publishing houses and markets them to bookstores, specialty stores, supermarkets, and newsstands for discount sale.

Inventory control is a chief problem at a company like Post. Turnover is high. It's essential to know exactly what is on hand, to get materials in, stored, and shipped as rapidly as possible, and to handle accounts efficiently. At a management task group meeting recently, you and the inventory control officer jointly proposed the purchase of computer terminals for several departments, including the warehouse. Under your direction, employees were given concentrated training in computer use and directed by their supervisors to cease manual procedures as rapidly as possible.

The decision couldn't have come at a better time. Business conditions have turned quite bad; together with the supervisors and upper management, you've just had to work out the furlough of several employees. You hope that the layoff will be brief, but it's hard to tell. At least you had the foresight to propose the computer terminals; you're looking good in the eyes of top management. The work can continue with a few less employees and may even be more efficient. Employees to be laid off were notified via letters in their time card slots this morning, August 8. The layoff will begin August 15.

Your secretary just brought in a phone message from Norman King, a supervisor, saying that you should expect a grievance from Steve Sandusky, the union's grievance committee chairman, over the layoff of Frank Carney in the warehouse. The union claims that Carney is more senior to an employee who is being retained.

You'll need to get in touch with King to get the details. You're mildly disturbed, since you thought that all this was covered in the supervisors' meeting. You told the supervisors that, in making their recommendations, their chief concern should be that the remaining employees could do the work. The contract was to be followed, but it does not require strict adherence to seniority if the remaining employees aren't qualified.

In any case, you'll have to be refreshed on the details concerning the warehouse. Your practice is to rely on the advice of your supervisors, who know their departments, when it comes to the operational implications of personnel actions.

Additional Relevant Information

ARTICLE III MANAGEMENT RIGHTS

Subject only to express limitations of this Agreement, the Company shall retain and exercise at its discretion the unqualified right to manage and to select and direct the work force. This right includes, but is not limited to: determination of products and methods; planning and scheduling; determining all job duties; assigning employees to jobs; hiring; transferring; promoting; disciplining for cause; suspending; discharging; laying off; rehiring; and issuing and enforcing rules, procedures and directives which do not conflict with this Agreement.

ARTICLE VII SENIORITY

A. The ordinary rules of seniority shall prevail with respect to furlough and recall. Plantwide seniority, as applied within Departments, shall govern the order of layoff and recall, providing that the remaining employee(s) is qualified to replace the laid off employee.

B. Official Department Lists will be maintained and posted for the three Departments, Field Drivers, Warehousemen, and Batch Plant Truck Drivers, showing the initial hire date and the date of Department appointment.

C. A two-year retention of seniority after layoff shall be observed.

DEPARTMENT LIST—WAREHOUSEMEN

Clock #	Hire Date	Dept. Appointment Date	Name
1211	3/5/65	3/5/65	HAPATIKA, Salvatore
1433	8/2/67	5/9/68	DAKOTA, Pierre S.
0901	9/9/69	6/2/74	FREUND, Amie
1018	10/1/69	4/8/72	CARNEY, Frank

EXCERPT: PLANTWIDE SENIORITY LIST

Clock #	Hire Date	Employee
0039	8/5/76	BALTHAZER, Douglas
1892	8/9/76	HALE, John
2089	9/1/76	SHORTS, James

Roles

UNION	MANAGEMENT
Witness	Two Foremen
Shop Committee Chairman	Manager, Labor Relations

Role of the Witness

Your name is William Barton. You have worked as a pipefitter for the Zadarak Fabricating Company for the past seven years. On March 2, you noticed two foremen, Wally Patrick and Dick Kogel, enter the cleaner-scrubber tank, which is visible from your work station. You had no reason to take note of the time, so you can't be certain when you saw them enter but, as best you can reconstruct it, the time was probably around 8:20 to 8:40 a.m. You know that it wasn't too long after the start of your shift at 8. About 9, you left your work station to get some additional tools in the storeroom and when you returned, sometime between 9:15 and 9:30, as best you can estimate the time, you noticed that they were still in the tank. You're not certain when they left, but they were gone when you took a coffee break at 10:30 and you think that they were probably there until after 10. The total time, then, as best you can recollect, may have been as much as an hour and a half or more.

Each time you did notice Patrick and Kogel in the tank, they were scraping and pounding all over the cleaner-scrubber. It seemed to you as if foremen shouldn't be doing such work when laborers were available. In fact, it was just one more instance of foreman doing bargaining unit work—something that seemed to be happening all the time. After lunch, laborers did come in to tear apart the cleaner-scrubber completely, apparently for a major overhaul. But from what you could see, laborers should have been in that tank, using picks and bars for the hour and a half in the morning when the foremen were doing the work instead.

At lunch, you contacted your zone committeeman, Emil Frank, to report the incident. Emil got a complete report from you to send to Steve Karpinsky, the shop committee chairman. Emil said that the union would definitely grieve.

Role of the Shop Committee Chairman

Your name is Steve Karpinsky. You are shop committee chairman for the union representing the employees of the Zadarak Fabricating Company. This afternoon, March 2, you received the following report from Zone Committeeman Emil Frank.

Steve—

163

Case 18:
Cleaned
Beyond
Inspection

Bill Barton, a pipefitter, reported to me during lunch that he observed two foremen, Wally Patrick and Dick Kogel, doing bargaining unit work this morning.

Barton says that the two foremen were in the cleaner-scrubber tank, where they spent as much as an hour and a half or more, by themselves, scraping and pounding the cleaner-scrubber. That afternoon, laborers were brought in to tear the unit apart for a complete overhaul.

Bill is hazy on the exact time that Patrick and Kogel were in the tank. But as best he can remember, it was between 8:20 and 8:40 when he saw them enter and probably after 10 when they left. He knows for certain that they were still in the tank around 9:15 or 9:30, when he returned from the storeroom.

This is just one more foreman-working grievance to add to the pile. They have absolutely no business using picks or bars and scraping and pounding on a piece of machinery. If foremen want to do an inspection to see what's wrong with a piece of machinery, fine. But if there's picking or scraping work to be done—even in the course of the inspection—they should be supervising laborers to do it. It's clear that they were trying to clean the cleaner-scrubber themselves to see if they could get it working and that they then did an elaborate inspection and even started tearing it down themselves.

This kind of thing is undermining our bargaining unit and we've got to put a stop to it somehow. There were 15 Laborers in the department working on the shift at that time, plus at least 50-60 eligible laborers on other shifts or on layoff who could have been called in to do the work. I think the grievance should seek 90 minutes pay each for the two senior laborers on the shift.

Emil

You agree completely with Frank's analysis. In the last year alone, the local has had to file over 100 foreman-working grievances. You file grievances with Earl Roberts, manager, labor relations. You told Emil Frank to inform the foremen that the union would be grieving at step 2.

Roles of the Foremen

Your names are Walter Patrick and Dick Kogel. Both of you are foremen at the Zadarak Fabricating Company. You learned this afternoon, March 2, that the union was filing a grievance against you for doing bargaining unit work in the cleaner-scrubber tank this morning. You both think that the grievance is ridiculous—one more example of harassment by the union. Layoffs have created major political problems with the union, and it has been going out of its way lately to file grievances, especially foremen-working grievances.

When you came on at 8 this morning, you got a report from the night turn foreman, Bill Neal, that the cleaner-scrubber began malfunctioning at the end of the shift and he had the line shut down. If the cleaner-scrubber doesn't work, there is a major backup in the fabrication process. It was essential that you determine the nature of the problem as soon as possible.

As soon as you got all laborers assigned and paperwork straightened, the two of you went to the cleaner-scrubber tank. Kogel brought along a crow bar in case needed for the inspection. You entered the tank shortly after 8:45 and began a visual inspection. It appeared that at least one of the rollers was improperly aligned. Kogel pried it off so that you could also look at the deflector plate, the bearings, and saddles. The deflector plate also appeared to be misaligned, but it was difficult to tell because of the buildup of chemicals, grease, and hardened gunk. It was obvious that a cleaning was long overdue, at least. But in order to tell if the plate itself had a problem, Kogel scraped off the gunk with the bar while Patrick examined the plate under a flashlight. Kogel noticed that the plate was cracked. You then jointly decided that the unit might as well be torn down for a complete overhaul, which would probably require a full shift.

Patrick then left the tank to return to the office to check the schedule and determine if sufficient Laborers would be available to tear the unit down, beginning in the afternoon. Kogel looked around for a few minutes more, then returned to the office to call the maintenance supervisor to arrange to have a millwright inspect the deflector plate. Kogel looked at his watch while on the phone and noted that it was 9:30. The total elapsed time that either or both of you were in the tank could not have been more than 35 to 40 minutes.

You had no intention of doing any cleaning or maintenance work. Your only purpose was to carry out an inspection to determine what had to be done with the cleaner-scrubber.

When you learned that a grievance would be filed, Kogel called Earl Roberts, manager, labor relations, to tell him about the grievance and to explain the background. Roberts said that he wanted to meet with you both late this afternoon to go over the details. He too said that he was tired of the union's harassment everytime a supervisor comes anywhere near a tool.

Role of the Manager, Labor Relations

Your name is Earl Roberts. You are manager, labor relations, at the Zadarak Fabricating Company. You learned this afternoon, March 2, that the union intends to file a grievance against Foremen Wally Patrick and Dick Kogel for doing bargaining-unit work. Kogel told you that the grievance was coming and filled you in a little on the details. You told him that you wanted to see both of them late this afternoon to get all of the details.

According to Kogel, the two foremen spent 30 to 40 minutes this morning in the cleaner-scrubber tank doing an inspection since the unit had malfunctioned on night shift. They had to do some scraping with a bar to find out the extent of the problem which turned out to be a cracked deflector plate. The whole unit has been shut down for complete overhaul, probably requiring a full shift. Apparently the union is claiming that the foremen shouldn't have used tools and that for anything other than a strict, hands-off, visual inspection, the foremen should have called in laborers.

You know that the union has political problems because so many men are laid off, but you're tired of this kind of harassment. They have filed over 100 foreman-working grievances in the last year, and nearly all of them are frivolous. In fact, you're waiting for it to come to the point where they file a grievance if a foreman picks up a discarded coffee cup from the floor and throws it in a trash can instead of calling in a janitor or laborer.

Steve Karpinsky, the union's shop committee chairman, usually presents the grievances. You still want to find out the details from Patrick and Kogel, but it looks like you'll all be involved in one more wasted grievance meeting.

Index

About the Authors

Donald S. McPherson is professor of labor relations and chairperson of the Graduate Department of Labor Relations at Indiana University of Pennsylvania. He is a practicing arbitrator listed on the American Arbitration Association labor panel, the Expedited Panel of the Coordinating Steel Companies—United Steelworkers of America, and the rosters of the Pennsylvania Bureau of Mediation and the Pennsylvania Labor Relations Board.

Professor McPherson holds a Ph.D. in labor history from the University of Pittsburgh. He has taught graduate courses in grievance resolution, employment discrimination, public sector labor relations, employee rights under law, and labor history, as well as undergraduate courses in collective bargaining. He is an associate director of the Pennsylvania Center for the Study of Labor Relations and regularly conducts short courses and training seminars for labor and management in grievance resolution and arbitration.

An experienced trainer, Professor McPherson has worked for industry, unions, utilities, health care facilities, educational institutions, and state and local government developing programs in the areas of communication skills, supervision, steward development, and equal employment opportunity. He previously has been employed as a personnel administrator and served as grievance chairman and president of his faculty union. He is active in the Industrial Relations Research Association, the Society of Professionals in Dispute Resolution, the University and College Labor Education Association, and the American Society for Personnel Administration.

Conrad John Gates is associate professor of labor relations in the Graduate Department of Labor Relations at Indiana University of Pennsylvania. He is a practicing arbitrator, listed on the Federal Mediation and Conciliation Service roster, the American Arbitration Association labor panel, the Expedited Panel of the Coordinating Steel Companies—United Steelworkers of America, and the rosters of the Pennsylvania Bureau of Mediation and the Pennsylvania Labor Relations Board.

Professor Gates holds a J.D. from the University of Buffalo School of Law. He has taught graduate courses in arbitration and advocacy, labor law, and employee rights under law and undergraduate courses in collective bargaining. He is an associate director of the Pennsylvania Center for the Study of Labor Relations and regularly conducts short courses and training seminars for labor and management in arbitration.

Professor Gates, formerly chairman of the Department of Business Administration at St. Vincent College, has been employed in a corporate legal department in the steel industry with responsibilities for labor relations and arbitration. He is a member of the American Arbitration Association and the Westmoreland County Bar Association.

Kevin N. Rogers has been employed as a personnel relations assistant in private industry. He has served as research assistant in the Graduate Department of Labor Relations at Indiana University of Pennsylvania and as assistant to the dean of the University of Pennsylvania School of Law.

Mr. Rogers earned an M.A. in labor relations from Indiana University of Pennsylvania and a B.A. in English from the University of Pennsylvania. He has assisted in conducting training workshops and conferences for the Pennsylvania Center for the Study of Labor Relations and is a member of the Industrial Relations Research Association and the American Society for Personnel Administration.